Global Endorsements for *A Divine Assignment*

From Africa

Dr David Emmanuel Goatley has done the church a great service by writing this book on one of the unsung heroes of modern missions. *A Divine Assignment: The Missiology of Wendell Clay Somerville* is a highly accessible missiology of one of the legendary missionaries to come out of the Baptist Tradition in America. The book will appeal to all those who take the task of global missions seriously. It speaks to both the missioner and missionised contexts. Through Goatley's book Wendell Somerville still speaks in a refreshing way that challenges all persons of faith with the "Divine Call."

Dr Henry J Mugabe
Principal, Baptist Theological Seminary of Zimbabwe

I used to wonder why Lott Carey Baptist Foreign Mission Society was so different from other mission organizations in its philosophy and practice on missions. When you read this book about the missional theology of Wendell Clay Somerville, you will definitely learn of the strength of Lott Carey. I was not privileged to meet this great giant, but after reading through the manuscript I feel like I know who Somerville was. David Emmanuel Goatley is, indeed, standing on the shoulders of the tall and strong man, and this book is a rich resource for leadership, missiology and theological studies. To Dr. Goatley, I say *"siya bonga mfowethu"*.

Rev. Ngwedla Paul Msiza
General Secretary, Baptist Convention of South Africa

From Asia Pacific

Some stories simply have to be told! David Goatley has captured the life, passions and missiology of Wendell Clay Somerville in an outstanding way. As a non-American who never had the privilege of meeting Dr Somerville, I'm captivated by his passion for the gospel, emboldened by his courage, challenged by his capacity and energized by his role model. This book not only tells the story of an outstanding missional leader; it also sets a benchmark for those who follow his lead.

Dr Briav Winslade
National Director Baptist Union of Australia

From the Caribbean

David Emmanuel Goatley provides a lucid exposé of the missiology of a church leader whose contribution deserves to be celebrated within the Baptist family and beyond. David plugs a gaping knowledge gap and meets a real need at a time when we observe in some sections of the ecclesial community a welcome renewal of awareness of the centrality of mission to the church's God-given vocation.

Rev. Neville Callam
General Secretary, Baptist World Alliance

From Europe

David Emmanuel Goatley's exploration of Wendell Clay Somerville's passionate and long leadership in global missions is not only a tribute of honour from one leader to another leader, but it is also a strong challenge for contemporary fellow Christians to respond faithfully to God's call to mission today. Somerville's long preaching ministry throughout so many crucial moments of the 20th century is a strong testimony of genuine faith, prophetic awareness, love for the church, and holistic vision of Christian missions. Almost every quotation of Somerville's words calls for a pause of meditation. His words call for conversion and nurture hope.

Rev. Anna Maffei
President, Unione Cristiana Evangelica Battista d'Italia

From North America

Prophetic leadership emerges from somewhere, and effective missional ministry is the result. David Emmanuel Goatley provides clear evidence of this as he unpacks the remarkable ministry of the missionary statesman, Wendell Clay Somerville. He illustrates that it is not the programs that are brought to the table that show the measure and character of a leader. It is the values and character that undergird them and the firm belief that the church can make a difference not just locally but globally. This is more than a biography, it is a missional footprint of how we shape ministry today.

Dr. Gary V. Nelson
General Secretary, Canadian Baptist Ministries
Vice President, Baptist World Alliance

A Divine Assignment is a fitting tribute to the life and legacy of Dr. Wendell Clay Somerville who served as the Executive Secretary of the Lott Carey Baptist Foreign Mission Convention for more than fifty years. David Emmanuel Goatley eloquently explores the missional thought and practice of his predecessor with penetrating words that clearly articulate his perspective and pathos for missional service. Every pastor and every believer should be inspired by the indefatigable commitment and lifestyle of this world class Christian for his lifelong commitment to the transformation of God's world.

Dr. Gina M. Stewart
Pastor, Christ Missionary Baptist Church
Memphis, Tennessee, USA

David Emmanuel Goatley has given us great insight into the theology and missiology of one the great missionaries of the 20th century. The Church is on mission, and where there is no mission there is no church. In this work, Dr. Goatley helps the reader to think through not only the historical accomplishments of Lott Carey but also the implication for missions in the 21st Century. Thank you, David, for advancing the Kingdom with this book.

Dr. Alyn E. Waller
Pastor, Enon Tabernacle Baptist Church
Philadelphia, Pennsylvania, USA

From South America

I'm grateful to my friend David Goatley for writing this book. Latin American Baptists do not know much about African American cultures or traditions. We know even less about African American Baptist Churches. This book helps us to know more about the African American Baptist missional tradition. This presentation of the thinking of Wendell Clay Somerville brings him alive to us and helps us to know him. It is only when we know each other as persons and when we know about common struggles and difficulties that we really can say that we relate and truly know one another as the family of God.

Pastor Raquel Contreras
Presidenta, Unión de Iglesias Evangélicas Bautistas de Chile
Vice President, Baptist World Alliance

A Divine Assignment

"The man of truth is in debt to the man who lacks truth.
The man of power is in debt to the man who is weak.
The man of wealth is in debt to the man without this
 world's good.
The man of education is in debt to the unlearned
 throughout the world.
The man who is filled is in debt to the man whose
 stomach is empty.
The man who has Christ as his Savior is in debt to the
 two-thirds of the human race who has never heard
 the glorious message of salvation."

Wendell Clay Somerville

A Divine Assignment

The Missiology of
Wendell Clay Somerville

David Emmanuel Goatley

LUCAS
PARK
BOOKS
ST. LOUIS, MISSOURI

ISBN: 978-1-60350-011-1

Published by Lucas Park Books
www.lucasparkbooks.com

Table of Contents

Acknowledgements

Exploring missional thought of Wendell Clay Somerville has been an exciting adventure. And as is the case with most of life, the journey is just as important as the destination, and the partners who travel with you are essential to the experience as well. Traveling this road of discovery and discernment has been enriched by many thoughtful Christian missional leaders who are part of the Lott Carey Baptist Foreign Mission Convention family, and I am indebted to all of them.

The talented and diverse network of international sisters and brothers who share leadership in the Lott Carey community have been incredibly important through this project. My colleagues in Africa, Asia, the Caribbean, Europe, North America, Oceania, and South America have encouraged me and provided formal and informal feedback that has enlarged my understanding of this important work. Many of them knew Wendell Clay Somerville. Some of them lived in the Somerville home with Wendell and his beloved wife, Alice during student years. Those who experienced him "up close and personal" have both taught me and learned from this evolving project. To each of them, I say "tatenda".

The wonderful people and churches that comprise the Lott Carey family in the United States are a joy to serve. Their historical disciplined focus on *helping churches extend their witness to the ends of the earth* and our contemporary commitment to *touching lives with the transforming love of Christ* continue to inspire and inform my ministry. Lott Carey leaders who served alongside Somerville and who shepherded the transition from his tenure to my term of leadership consistently modeled the management of change marvelously. From my election to succeed Somerville in November 1996 through my orientation and transition months to my formal assumption of full-time responsibilities on 1 June 1997, these leaders have been mentors, colleagues, and friends. While several people played essential roles in helping to graft me into the Lott Carey movement, I am especially grateful to John H. Foster (who chaired the Search Committee that recommended my call), Norman W. Smith, Sr. (now Chairman Emeritus of Lott Carey's Executive Board and Executive Committee) and Chauncey R. Edwards (former Lott Carey President, former Special Assistant to Somerville, and Interim Executive Secretary-Treasurer prior to my call). They and their colleagues modeled thoughtful, faithful, and orderly transition worthy of emulation.

The members of churches in the Lott Carey network who pray, give, and go on mission with Christ in the Spirit throughout God's world are wonderful people. They are ordinary people who do extraordinary work. Their compassion for people near and far warm the spirit and encourage faithful service. Their commitment to the Gospel of Jesus Christ in word and deed around the world are greatly inspirational. They assure me that I am in their prayers, and they remember the sacrifices that my family makes for the sake of the Gospel. This great host of witnesses is invaluable to the impact of the Lott Carey community.

I am blessed to be part of a loving and nurturing family. Wilbert Goatley, Sr. (my pastor who led my spiritual formation), Lillian Goatley (my late mother who taught me more about the love of God than anyone), and Verlene Goatley (my stepmother whose service as a missionary in Liberia and whose ministry of prayer encourages me); Wilbert Goatley, Jr. (my brother whose thoughtful pastoral and scholarly insights expand me) and Shirley Duncan (my sister who modeled Christian hospitality as graciously as I ever knew); and Pamela (my wife who brings me strength for today) and Atiba Emmanuel (my son who gives me hope for tomorrow) have planted and watered seeds of love that sustain me through the sometimes struggles of global missional service.

Finally, the faithful disciples of Jesus who are part of our staff based in the United States deserve more affirmation than they ever receive. Thankfully, they do not work for fame and recognition (nor the money they deserve). We all pull heavy loads and do the work of two, three, and more people on a regular basis. I am fortunate to have worked with a number of committed Christian leaders who work in the background and foreground to help us help one another to live into God's will for our lives. For my present domestic staff colleagues and for those who have worked in early years, I am grateful.

To all who enable me to lead and to learn, I say, "zicomo"!

David Emmanuel Goatley
Washington, DC, USA
2010

Foreword

Twenty years ago historian Sandy Martin produced a monumental work entitled *Black Baptists and African Missions*, detailing the missionary history of former slaves returning or turning to their native land. His thesis involved these basic assertions:

That black Christians in general and black Baptists in particular actively engaged in an effort to evangelize Africa during the late nineteenth and early twentieth centuries; that they understood redemption or salvation of non-Christian Africans in material or temporal as well as spiritual terms; that this enterprise demonstrated their sense of racial identity with all peoples of African descent; . . . and that this missionary quest on behalf of the ancestral homeland contributed to the development of and conflicts among black Baptist denominations.[1]

David Emmanuel Goatley's intriguing study of the work of the Lott Carey Baptist Foreign Mission Convention, as seen through the career of its longtime executive secretary Wendell Clay Somerville, clearly demonstrates the truth of Martin's thesis. Born in 1897 of denominational divisions over the nature and practice of the Christian mission, the Lott Carey Baptist Foreign Mission Society was founded to evangelize the world, beginning in Africa. It linked the conversion of the human heart to the alleviation of human need, extending racial "connectedness" in ways that drew Africans and African Americans back to their shared roots and common ancestors.

Lott Carey (d. 1829) was a Virginia slave who bought back his freedom in 1813 and poured himself into the church's missionary calling. Sent to Africa in 1821 by the American Baptist Board of Foreign Missions, Carey founded the Providence Baptist Church and school in Monrovia in what became the colony of Liberia. Working tirelessly to offer a Christian witness in West Africa, Carey later became vice governor and acting governor of Liberia1828-29.[2]

The Lott Carey Baptist Foreign Mission Society began in 1897 as a result of deepening commitments to missional theology and practice among African American Baptists and disputes over the specific mission strategy promoted by they newly formed National Baptist Convention (1895). Like many Baptist endeavors, the initial phase this missionary enterprise was punctuated by strong personalities and inevitable schism. The founders of this new mission organization, many based in Virginia, took the name of Lott Carey and set their initial sights on Africa. Today the Lott Carey Baptist Foreign Mission Convention is one of the great Protestant mission agencies worldwide with an abiding concern for the Church in Africa and with global networks and strategies for the future. To understand the work of the Lott Carey Convention, one must give careful attention to the contribution of Wendell Clay Somerville (1900-1997) who served as the Convention's executive secretary and treasurer for some fifty-five years, 1940-1995. Somerville, often overlooked by students of African American Baptist history and Christian missions in the United States, shaped the Convention and its missional identity in powerful and insightful ways. His theology of the Gospel's missionary imperative is explored insightfully in the volume by David Emmanuel Goatley, Somerville's successor as chief executive of the Lott Carey Convention.

Such a study is important for several reasons. First, Wendell Clay Somerville was an outstanding leader in American Protestantism in general and in African American Protestantism in particular. Until the publication of this book, his missional theology has never been as fully explored. Second, his contribution inside African American Baptist life has been greatly overlooked. It is time to examine his approach to missions and the impact of his views on the Lott Carey Convention and its network of congregations.

Third, since Somerville's life and work spanned the entire twentieth century, his varying approaches to the theological and organizational impetus for Christian missions inside and outside the African American Baptist community is extremely important. It offers insights into the changing nature of global mission theory and practice from the beginning of the Second World War to the edge of the twenty-first century. Those years witnessed the rise of a truly global international culture and connectedness, a reality that both challenged and informed proponents of the church's missional imperative such as Wendell Clay Somerville. Fourth, Somerville's long tenure bridged numerous cultural transitions in American racial and religious life from the segregationist society of Jim Crow to the successes and continued struggles of the Civil Rights Movement. His steady and creative effort to extend the Christian gospel amid the racial realities and changes of his times is itself a study in Christian grace and hope. Finally, Somerville's missional vision blends Biblicism, spirituality, theology, and ministry in ways that may continue to impact a global vision of the church's mission for the future. His commitments to evangelical witness and tangible response to human suffering are important models for continued missional integrity in a pluralistic, post-modern world. Surely, Lott Carey, ex-slave, Baptist preacher and global visionary, would have been pleased.

Bill J. Leonard
Dean and Professor of Church History
The Divinity School
Wake Forest University

Introduction

Wendell Clay Somerville is one of the 20th Century's most important missiologists. This book explores some of the theological insights that contributed to his effective leadership of the Lott Carey Baptist Foreign Mission Convention, the premier African American global missions agency of his era. It is impossible to give a comprehensive assessment of his missiology that emerged during more than one-half century of global Christian missions leadership in these few pages. This work, however, introduces some of the critical concepts and commitments of one of the most significant missional leaders of the contemporary church. They are instructional, and they are inspirational. They are useful for the robust missional life of the 21st Century church.

Some will ask why they have not heard of Wendell Somerville if he is as important as I claim him to be. In the words of a pastor colleague of mine, "There are no great preachers; only good preachers greatly exposed." This is the case with Somerville. Regrettably, he has not enjoyed broad exposure in the American church arena nor the global missional field. Further, Somerville concentrated on leading the missions community to which he was called and on communicating his message and vision within that circle. He did not seek to publicize his work in the face of the

1

segregated United States missional, academic, or publishing networks nor in their marginally improved climates in the aftermath of successes from the civil rights struggle. The time has come for wider exposure to this global Christian leader.

Somerville was highly esteemed in the constituency of the Lott Carey Baptist Foreign Mission Convention until the dawn of the 21st Century, and this is a sizeable community that now comprises some 3,000 churches. He was a living legend in the minds of some. His relentless prioritization for missions in the Two-thirds World, his Christian integrity, his personal character, and his near obsession with frugality in order to maximize direct missional investments combined to produce great respect. He was one of those unique people who could even garner respect from those who did not particularly like his personality and idiosyncrasies. According to one of his near contemporaries, "I never did like the man, but I respected him and supported him."

Somerville concentrated on doing his work rather than talking about his work. This is the case of most African American Christian leaders. While the tide is now changing for some, most of us concentrate on getting the job done rather than getting the word out. This preoccupation with "walking" and an inattention to "talking" has prevented the global Christian community from knowing as much about black Christian leadership as it should. Consequently, we are all impoverished by the gaping holes that exist in the history of the church's witness in the world. This brief introduction to the missional thought of Wendell Somerville is a modest effort to help bridge a part of that gap.

Wendell Clay Somerville attributed his ministry as the principal leader of "the only distinct Foreign Mission Convention among Negroes in the world"[1] to God's providence. God's hand had guided the formation of the Lott Carey Baptist Foreign Mission Society (Lott Carey) in 1897. God had inspired its leaders and constituency to focus consistently on missions outside the United States of America. God had kept Lott Carey as a leading community of American Negro Baptist Churches. God had called Somerville to the awesome task of assuming the organization's executive office.

Beyond understanding God's providential hand in the formation and maturation of Lott Carey, Somerville saw his call to its executive office as a unique privilege of service. Despite the fact that his father was among the founding members of the organization and his uncle was its first president, Somerville did not articulate a sense of inheritance. He did not assume he was destined to be a leader of the Lott Carey community. He held quite the opposite position. Throughout his 55 years of leadership, he constantly communicated a deep sense of honor that God would favor him and that the Lott Carey leaders and constituents would affirm him as the executive leader of such a significant community. As he reflected on 50 years as the chief executive officer of Lott Carey, he referred to his responsibilities, as he had done in numerous sermons throughout the years, as "my divine assignment."[2]

By today's standards, Somerville can sound condescending when writing of persons in Two-Thirds World contexts. He uses language of the "needy" and "native" easily. It is unfair, however, to criticize him for being a person of his era. While many correctly seek to avoid this kind of language today, it was common usage for a missional leader born in 1900. Despite the language that causes concern when held to contemporary standards, Somerville's tone in speaking of the "needy" and the "native" was balanced by the tenderness and humility with which he viewed his role and the roles of missionaries under his leadership. Hear his humility: "When I think of the sacrifices and hardships which these natives, teachers and preachers are daily making for the extension of the Kingdom, I count my feeble efforts of service but refuse."[3]

When he speaks of the contributions of education and evangelism in Haiti made by Catherlene Shaw and Annie E. Bowers, principal and assistant principal respectively of Lott Carey's school in St. Marc, he admiringly writes,

A modern miracle has been wrought by these two godly young women. They have brought to this school all of their scientific and modern pedagogical knowledge and experience. ... These teachers have introduced the revolutionary attitude of love into Haiti. I had been previously told that one must be exact, stern, and even "hard" in dealing with these natives. Now I can realize how outmoded this idea is. Human nature is the same everywhere. There is no force in dealing with humanity, as powerful as that of love and sympathy. These young women have literally won the hearts of these poor humble people of Haiti.[4]

By 1943, Boaz A. Harris had served as the superintendent for Lott Carey's missionary work in Haiti for 22 years and had 80 stations under his supervision. Responding to their own desperate need for a church building in St. Marc, the community with whom Harris worked raised nearly eight hundred dollars ($800.00) from their own meager incomes. News of this significant effort inspired Lott Carey leaders to appeal for additional gifts of "at least ten dollars ($10.00) toward this special effort." Lott Carey board members responded so substantially that 1,000 bags of cement were sent from the U.S. With the collaboration of the White Rock Baptist Church in Durham, N.C., which donated property it owned in St. Marc to Lott Carey, the Convention and its Haitian partners were able to proceed toward erecting a church building. Speaking of the leadership of Boaz Harris, Somerville recorded:

Dr. Harris and his devoted family have been called upon to make brick without straw for twenty-two years. The hardships and disappointments were sufficient to discourage almost anyone, but because of his faith in God and faith in the possibilities of this great host of unwashed humanity, he has remained at his post of duty and now, thank God, a way has been opened whereby his prayers and efforts are about to be rewarded. Dr. Harris has completely lost himself in the task which has been assigned him. Because of his Christian fortitude, spirit of sincerity and energetic work, he has won the respect of all classes of people in Haiti.[5]

Somerville repeatedly confessed his gratitude for the privilege of his missional leadership opportunities. Sharing with Christ in reconciling the world to God brought him great joy, and he executed his duties with much enthusiasm. His work with missionaries around the world humbled him, and working in partnership with those who labored in often overwhelmingly challenging contexts gave additional cause for him to rejoice.

Wendell Somerville also celebrated his citizenship and was grateful for the opportunities afforded him and other Americans. He was an American patriot. By patriot, I mean one who supports one's country and works toward it's becoming its best that it can be, as opposed to one who naively affirms its alleged faultlessness and romanticizes its uneven history. He was not blind to the blemishes on the American record. He was a stern critic of the racism that contaminated so much of the American spirit. Yet he was committed to the United States. Further, he was a tireless advocate of seeking the full inclusion of African Americans in all levels of the national experience and international engagements. As a Christian who was an American, Somerville stressed that the American task was "to apply the ethical principles of Jesus Christ so that our economic system may be moralized, our industrial relationships may be humanized, our international relationships may be civilized, our racial relationship Christianized, and that justice saturate our laws and legislation."[6]

In his own words, he had "love and devotion to America and the fundamental principles upon which she is founded."[7] An expression of his concern for his country was related to his distress about the reach and scope of Communism he found in Southeast Asia in 1960. He echoed contemporary concerns of the creeping Communism of China into Vietnam as well as Laos. He was certain the people of Cambodia also were vulnerable to the threat of Communism. The burden he felt after visiting Southeast Asia led Somerville to write the following letter.

December 21, 1960

Honorable Chester Bowles
The Under Secretary of State
Washington, DC

My dear Mr. Bowles:

My wife and I have recently returned to the United States after completing an around-the-world tour. Our visit carried us to several countries throughout Africa, the Middle East and Asia.

The purpose of our trip was to study and review the general missionary and educational programs throughout these areas; and to evaluate our own particular program in these regions.

As we talked with some leaders and numerous people in various walks of life, we observed that the people throughout these regions respect the United States because of her economic progress and her military strength. However, we also found that there is a deep reservoir of goodwill lying untapped throughout Asia and Africa.

It is our considered opinion that America has a great opportunity to win the genuine love and friendship of these people if she would take the bold venture of carefully selecting some of its qualified American Negroes and send them into these regions as representatives of the American Government. There are several American Negroes whose character, training, and intellectual achievements would thoroughly tap this reservoir of goodwill and understanding.

Such American Negroes as Dr. Mordecai W. Johnson, Judge William Hastie, Attorney Thurgood Marshall, Dr. Rayford Logan, just to name a few, are persons fully qualified to represent American Democracy through the world.

We were in India on November 9, 1960 when news came of the election of Senator John F. Kennedy to the Presidency of the United States. Thousands of these people rejoiced because they felt that you would return to a policy-making position in the Cabinet of the New Administration; and these people regard you as one of

*the great statesmen of this generation in your understanding of the
desires and yearnings of your fellowman.*

*My purpose in addressing this letter to you is the hope that
you will use your good office in presenting the urgency in having
qualified American Negroes appointed to positions of trust during
the New Administration.*

*With the hope that you will look with favor upon this petition;
and will seek to share your insight and interest in human relations
with the New Administration. I am*

Sincerely yours,
Wendell C. Somerville

Somerville viewed the entirety of his global missions
ministry as being lived in the midst of global catastrophe.
He expressed this sentiment in the 1940s in reference to
the cataclysmic events of World War II and continued to
communicate this outlook throughout the 1990s. He saw in
each decade great tragedies that threatened the welfare of the
entire earth and particularly exacerbated the struggles of the
poor and vulnerable around the world. He was committed
to missions against the backdrop of human uncertainty.
"Of course the Officials of the Lott Carey Baptist Foreign
Mission Convention remain cognizant and alert to the Good
News of adventure and boundless dimensions, yet we know
that it is a moment where might often substitutes morality;
and illness and poverty still stalk the majority of the human
race."[8]

Beginning in the 1990s with his fiftieth anniversary in
leadership of Lott Carey, Somerville's contributions in his
annual report took a decidedly reflective tone. He seems
to reminisce about his call from God to his post of service
and of his place of "watering" seeds planted by a succession
of faithful predecessors. He testifies of not being tired of
serving. His contributions are very brief. In announcing his
retirement from Lott Carey after 55 years of devoted service
to his "divine assignment" at age 95, Somerville recorded in
his final report as Executive Secretary-Treasurer of the Lott
Carey Baptist Foreign Mission Convention in 1995 these
penetrating words that summarize his perspective on his
life of missional service:

God has wonderfully blessed me to reach 95 glorious years of age; and although the infirmities of the past year have resulted in weariness of flesh and weakness of limbs, in a spiritual sense, "I don't feel no ways tired." I am glorifying God for electing me early to be a witness of his truth and permitting me to be a waterer of the Lott Carey seed that was planted back in 1897, and allowing me to enjoy much of the increase that only he can give. ... My daily prayer shall be that God will ever shower his blessings upon the officials and constituents of Lott Carey and whomever my successor may be; that the mission work may be extant and spread to the far-reaching corners of the earth; that those who are faint may be stirred; that those who are willing may be directed; that those who waver may be confirmed; that wisdom and integrity may be given to all, and that all things be ordered unto God's own glory."[9]

This book has three main movements. First, I present something of the insights Wendell Somerville had about the missional church. Somerville was an unabashed advocate of the global missional priority of the local church. In this approach, missions is not optional. It is essential. This section presents something of the high aspirations that Somerville has for the church, the impact he sees the church can make, and his frustration with those who keep the church from living up to its potential.

Second, I share a glimpse of Somerville's understanding of the missional life. Every Christian is called to missional living. The missional life, however, does not evolve out of ingenuity of individual effort. The missional life is an outgrowth of the transformation one experiences through faith in Jesus Christ as the Son of the Living God. The saved life opens one to the missional life. The missional life leads one to invest one's being in bringing a holistic Christian witness to a hurting world.

Third, I offer a summary of Somerville's missional strategy for the world. Missions for Somerville was evangelical and holistic. Experiencing the transforming power of Christ leads individuals and churches to engage the world for good. This involves a commitment to empowering people who live at the margins around the world to have more humane lives and to help the oppressed. His African American Christian heritage shaped his vision of Christ for the world with a particular interest in Africa. His vision was influenced by his ethnicity but not limited by it.

I have the unique privilege of being Somerville's immediate successor in leadership for the Lott Carey family. I regret that I only met him briefly twice before his death in 1997. The first meeting was when I was taken to his home to be introduced as his successor in April 1997. Upon learning this news, the aged and frail Somerville became quite pensive. The second meeting was upon my installation as the Executive Secretary-Treasurer of the Lott Carey organization in August the same year. In bidding him farewell as he exited the meeting, he shook my hand and said, "You've had a fine program today. Congratulations." This stunned me because it appeared that Somerville was physically present but not mentally alert to the proceedings. His words were a benediction on my life. I experienced a blessing in a deeply spiritual way that also brought a physical awareness of something significant being given to me.

I did not know Wendell Somerville while he led the Lott Carey organization. The longer I stand on his shoulders, however, the more I appreciate his adeptness as a missional and organizational leader. The peculiarities about him so frequently told to me in earlier years have long ceased to seem so eccentric. While all good leaders have their share of eccentricities, there was much method to the madness of Somerville the leader. However, reading hundreds of his sermons and pages of his missional writings has allowed me to know him better than anyone else currently alive. The more I read his sermons and writings, the more I came to marvel at his insight and his prophetic vision for missions and global events. He clearly understood the insanity of ever increasing nuclear and conventional weapons. He anticipated the growing strength of Japan. He understood the unwise foreign policy positions toward China and the consequential damage to the Christian witness that resulted. He grasped the critical opportunity for global leadership from African countries if they could negotiate coordinated economic and political collaboration. He also anticipated the likely interference from other economic and political forces that desired to exploit African disunity. He was a forward thinker and, in many ways, far ahead of his time.

I hope this book does not become the first and last word on the life and thought of Wendell Clay Somerville. There is much more work for those who will explore the layers of complexity and nuance in his work. He has much to teach us about the missional essence of the church and what Christ has given to all who follow him—"a divine assignment."

The Missional Church

The monumental changes of the 20th Century affected every aspect of people's lives. Governments, societies, congregations, families, and individuals were impacted in deep and lasting ways. Despite the rapid changes that were inevitable for all, Wendell Clay Somerville had an abiding confidence in the will of God for his life and for the lives of those who follow Jesus. He believed people would realize God's design for their lives as they were faithful to God's will in the world.

Somerville held that when the church is living faithfully as a community of God's people, it is sure of its destiny in the eternal will of God. It lives with a certainty of experiencing God's will for being witness to Christ in all of the earth. It lives with confidence because of the presence and guidance of the Holy Spirit in spite of the rapid changes and uncertainties of contexts around it. While the church inevitably errs and fails because of human fallibility, it also lives with an ultimate expectancy of victory because its future is bound up in the will of God, the presence of Christ, and the power of the Spirit.

Love and the Holy Spirit

Because of its confidence in God's plans for its life, the church is sure of its mission "to exalt the name of Christ everywhere and to persuade all [people] to accept him as their Lord and master." [1] The church does not embark on this audacious endeavor of its own ingenuity, however. The complimentary encounters with of love and the Holy Spirit enable and empower the church to realize its destiny in the will of God. They are indispensable.

The love of God causes the church to make Christ known around the world. The love that Somerville described as essential for the church is the self-giving love of God in Christ. This love inspires the church to invest its life and its resources for the good of others around the world— especially among those who do not know God through Jesus Christ, the impoverished, the unlearned, and the sick. As he matured and came to witness the exploitation of the poor by the rich in their own countries and across borders, he would come to include those that are frustrated by oppression among those to whom the church must express a liberating love. In God's community, Somerville asserted, people take rank according to their love and service.

Love leads those in God's community to value each person. The weakest are important. Those with handicaps are respected. Those in need receive care and understanding. Love enables us to see people as God sees them. Love led Somerville to believe in the full equality of all of humanity. He rejected the notion that some have greater value than others do. All people have the same basic physical needs, the need for meaningful relationships, and the spiritual yearning to become all they can be.

The value of humanity is confirmed by the love of God to us. The care and compassion of Christ for humanity demonstrates our great worth. Our judgment of ourselves is often that we are only a confused mass of humanity. God's estimate of human importance, however, is much higher. Our shallow reasoning cannot adequately assess the significance of human life.[2]

Jesus' view of humanity is radically different from much of humanity's view of various members of its own family. Somerville lamented the segmentation between the "haves" and the "have nots." He noted the peculiarity of identifying portions of the world's population as First World, Second World, and Third World. He noted how some privileged persons would label less fortunate people as "basket cases" because of their saturation in poverty, famine, and frustration. How odd it was to him that the richest people on earth in the United States allowed prosperity and selfishness to produce cultures of crime, disrespect, corruption, and materialism. The self-absorption of U.S. culture yielded a mindset of self-centeredness that led to a conclusion like that of the disciples to Jesus in Mark 6, to "send them away." The logical consequence of this preoccupation with self-interest has led to deeper and broader experiences of loneliness and lostness. Rather than living detached from things, people have become detached from others who live in need of compassion.[3] Ultimately, Somerville argued that "the strength and influence of a church are determined by what it does for others."[4] This strength and influence are driven by love.

The Holy Spirit is likewise essential for the church to have a credible witness in the world for Christ. Along with love's inducement to service is the presence and power of the Holy Spirit. Somerville contended that the anointing of the Holy Spirit is prerequisite for achieving the mission of the church. It is only after the Holy Spirit comes upon the church that it can live into its Christ-given mission.

The Holy Spirit empowers the Christian to be a credible witness to the world. The Spirit transforms life from self-centeredness to faithful surrender to the cause of Christ. Somerville claimed that Christians have a good case to present to the world through the Gospel of Jesus Christ. The problem is that many good cases are lost because of bad witnesses. In an interesting insight, Somerville claimed that the whole world sought reconciliation between well-fed Christians and, in contrast, the overwhelming number of hungry people. Comfortable Christians awkwardly stand out against those who are exploited and manipulated because of disproportionate distributions of power. People in the alleged "safe" church were contrasted against the lost and vulnerable in every part of the world. Somerville asserted that it was impossible to offer hope and help for the world without the power of the Holy Spirit. Without the power of the Holy Spirit, the people that claimed to be part of the church damaged the credibility of the Gospel.[5]

When the church is enveloped in love and the Spirit, the church can live into its destiny of bringing people into relationship with God through Jesus Christ. Somerville proclaimed:

> When the church is sure enough in action, she can face a hostile world and say that she has been baptized with the blood of the martyrs and glorified by deeds of supreme devotion and sacrifice. She has been the Mother of saints, sages, heroes, the builders of Cathedrals, churches, and institutions of sacred learning. She has been the Inspirer of art and poetry, Upholder of morality and social order, Pioneer of new and daring enterprises throughout the world. She has met with indifference and opposition, but even the gates of hell have not prevailed against her.
>
> Yes, at times she has been stained by sin, betrayed by her own leaders, rent by schisms, disgraced by deceits, compromised with evil, corrupted by pride and self-suffering, weakened by self-interest and self-complacency. With all of these admitted defects, she still gained an ever renewed hold upon the allegiance of [people], and has accomplished a redeeming and purifying and uplifting mission in Africa, Asia, and throughout the world among lost humanity that stirs the gratitude, enkindles the imagination, and evokes the loyalty of all who know something of what the church has meant to [humanity].[6]

Jerusalem Christians

Somerville cited the difficulty many churches had with maintaining a focus on global missions. He essentially saw this struggle resulting from a shallow faith. He saw too many "faithless" people standing in the way of the missional progress of the church. Their opposition to robust missional engagement, he surmised, was grounded in doubt. "They don't have faith in the faith they do have" was a memorable turn of phrase for Somerville. Weak faith disabled people from seeing the breadth of God's love for the world and from discerning the accompanying priority the church should have for the world. The world mission of the church requires heroism in the face of apparent defeat.[7]

The great need of the church of Somerville's day was to set aside people to do the work that no other agents, groups, or individuals could do—exalt the name of Jesus Christ in the entire world and persuade people to surrender their lives to him. This is what the *Acts of the Apostles* records that the church did with Barnabas and Paul, and it distinguished the church from all other well meaning and well serving humanitarian entities. Barnabas' and Paul's visions and concerns were too large to be contained with numerous local affairs. Their commission was global in scope. Somerville longed for churches that embraced global visions rather than local preoccupations.[8]

Christians with a preoccupation for their local "church work" were considered "Jerusalem Christians" by Somerville. He lamented that too many Christians majored in polishing brass around the temple rather than proclaiming the Gospel around the world. He noted that the spread of Christianity throughout the world did not emerge from the intentionality of the church leaders at Jerusalem. Christianity spread because of the persecution of the church in Jerusalem. "Up to this time, not a single official preacher had become sufficiently missionary-minded to leave the comforts of Jerusalem."[9]

Were the church to be dependent upon the example of the church leaders in Jerusalem, the Christian enterprise would have suffered tremendously.

Referring to the Acts 8:14 passage where after hearing that Samaria had accepted God's message, the Apostles at Jerusalem send Peter and John, Somerville observed that "many of our churches today are simply waiting to hear a message from Washington or London before they are awakened out of their slumber."[10] He further contended: "If these Apostles had taken Jesus seriously they would not have waited until a persecution drove others from their homes out into foreign fields as evangelists, but they would have voluntarily set forth with the word of life to the lost souls outside of comfortable Jerusalem."[11]

In many places he criticized churches of his day for their lack of global missionary zeal. Too many of them preferred to engage in local activities that were self-serving and unchallenging rather than to take on the task of carrying the Gospel everywhere. In this way he echoes the sentiments of Rev. Lott Carey, for whom the Lott Carey Convention is named. Carey was born enslaved in 1780, professed faith in Jesus Christ in 1807, purchased his freedom in 1813, and led the first Baptist missionary team to West Africa from the United States in 1821. Prior to leaving Norfolk, Virginia for Liberia where he served as a missional leader, he said:

> I feel it my duty to go, and I very much fear, that many of those who preach the gospel in this country, will blush when the Savior calls them to give an account of their labors in his cause, and tells them, 'I commanded you to go into all the world, and preach the gospel to every creature;' ... the Savior may ask, where have you been? Where have you been? What have you been doing? Have you endeavored to the utmost of your ability to fulfill the commands I gave you? Or have you sought your own gratification, and your own ease, regardless of my commands?[12]

Carey's sentiments presage Somerville's interpretation of the universal outreach of God's plan in Paul and Barnabus' lives (see Acts 16).

> According to God's plan, Paul and Barnabus had completed the preaching missions in Asia Minor, and now God's blueprint led Paul to "explore higher altitudes." This was the new arena where they could seek beyond themselves and experience what they could not derive from themselves.

The current tragedy is that so many of our preachers and leaders are so fascinated, charmed, and bewitched by the handclapping worshippers at Lystra and Derbe that they are unable to extricate themselves from the enchanting garlands and oxen. Many are religiously unable to see or feel beyond the narrow pigeonhole of their little congregations. This very littleness will ultimately bring the larger world vision down around their heads. These worshipers of Lystra and Derbe want everything to be their size. As a matter of fact, the religion of Lystra and Derbe is nothing more than a safe escape from the hard facts of God's word.[13]

World Evangelism

"The business of the church," argued Somerville "is to save souls and make him known throughout the world."[14] The strategy of making Christ known to all people everywhere was a holistic enterprise to him. Classical evangelism was essential. Communicating with people what God had uniquely done for the world through the life, death, and resurrection of Jesus was paramount. Empowerment, however, was likewise essential. People who lived in poverty and desperation required training that would enable them to make meaningful contributions to their communities and to the Kingdom of God in the world. Humanitarian efforts were indispensable. Healing the sick, feeding the hungry, clothing the naked, and the like were non-negotiable expectations from Christ to be carried out by his disciples.[15]

Early in his career at Lott Carey, Somerville sometimes struggled in the tension of the innumerable needs of people around the world, the tremendous opportunities available for missional engagement by his constituents, and the difficulty of stimulating adequate spiritual, personal, and financial resources to address the needs. "One of the painful tasks of being an Executive Secretary of a Foreign Mission Convention," he lamented, "is to possess such a large accumulation of facts and information about the miserable condition of people of other lands and, yet, you seem helpless in arousing so-called Christians at home to the sufferings of others."[16] While all missional Christian leaders live with similar struggles, Somerville' agony was particularly acute because of the global breadth of his vision for the mission of the church juxtaposed with the narrow worldviews of so many Christian leaders and, consequently, the congregations they led.

Somerville saw the church at Antioch as the model of a great church. This church was characterized by worship, the guidance of the Holy Spirit, and a broad outreach. He saw in this church an ideal blueprint for all future churches. In contrast to churches of his era that were divided in ways that robbed it of its power, "no group has ever set out with a greater racial, economic, and religious complexity than these unlearned and weaponless Christians who may be regarded as a 'colony of heaven.'"[17] He did not understand the biblical model of the church described in Antioch primarily as a group of people with an organized religious life in a local community. To the contrary, he understood the church to be "a community of God's people where [they] take rank according to their love and service."[18]

Somerville valued highly several unique qualities of this church. Their unity of the Spirit enabled a common action of witness for Christ. Their shared possessions prevented inequalities of wealth that he believed to be bases for wars and conflicts at national, community, and personal levels. They shared a common identity of being part of the human race. Their common identity was superior to a notion of "race" as an overarching social construct of the world that he lived in which he claimed was "the greatest enemy to Christianity today. … Race prejudice has robbed the church of its spiritual power." Finally, the Antioch Church shared a common commitment of sharing the Gospel with all people everywhere. He proclaimed,

> Not only did this little band of Christians take an offering for the weak church in Jerusalem, but they obeyed the voice of the Holy Spirit and sent forth

their TWO BEST MEN (emphasis in the original) to the foreign field, Paul and Barnabus. ...

Foreign missions is the heart of the New Testament church, and if we would recover the sprit of that First New Testament church, we must reexamine our religious thinking.[19]

Missional Failure

Somerville believed that much of the social, economic, political, and racial storms that his generation experienced could be attributed to the missional failure of much of the church. Inspired by the story of Jonah who went west toward Joppa in defiance of God's call for him to go east toward Nineveh and the great storm that engulfed the ship that he had boarded, Somerville called on the church of his era to confess their complicity in bringing the storm upon their environs.[20]

In a brief glance over the past year of 1963, we saw Medgar Evans shot down. We saw four little children blown into bits while attending Sunday school. We watched two determined and frightened men [Premier of the Soviet Union, Nikita Khrushchev and President of the United States, John F. Kennedy] face to face knowing that each had the power to push a button which would annihilate all plant and animal life. On November 22 the young dynamic President [John F. Kennedy] was shot down by a mad assassin's bullets. For the first time in recent history we have seen a man [Lyndon B. Johnson] who comes from the undemocratic southland elevated to the highest office of this land. Never has any generation lived in such fear and apprehension of total destruction by forces which man seems powerless to control.

... The church itself is largely responsible for much of the world problems through its doubts, vacillation, and prejudice. ... Billy Graham visited an African home in Calabar, Nigeria. His host showed him a newspaper article in which Graham's local pastor in North Carolina said, 'Whoever heard of a Negro preacher having anything to say to a white congregation?' ...The Dutch Reformed Church of South Africa supports the government policy of apartheid." [21]

Referring to the narrative in Acts 3 where Peter and John encounter a handicapped man who daily sat at the temple and was healed through the name of Jesus Christ, Somerville saw a significant challenge for the church in his era. He recognized people with substantive challenges in every aspect of life sitting daily "at the gates" of the churches of his day. He saw a helpless world in need. His was a world in which many lived frustrated with various political inequities. His was a world in which the majority of the population was impoverished. His was a world of depravity where families lived on the streets of urban cities. His was a world where massive numbers of people were constantly hungry. His was a world in which most people did not have the joy of the Gospel of Jesus shared with them. His world offered a challenge for the church to say to those that suffered and struggled, "Look on us." He called the church to rise to the challenge. The church may not have offered what people wanted. But it had what people needed.[22]

The world is full of tragedies that make human life miserable for some and unbearable for others. However, Somerville's thought holds that the world's greatest tragedy "is the fact that the so-called followers of Jesus have failed to use the spiritual resources to heal a broken and sick world which Christ has made possible. ... The [world's] greatest tragedy is the indifference of so-called Christians regarding their refusing to exalt the name of Jesus everywhere."[23] Any church that fails to focus on Jesus' program of seeking to save every person everywhere ceases to be a witness to the salvific power of the Gospel of Jesus Christ.[24] Emphasizing the truly global nature of missional people, he asserted, "A gospel that doesn't go everywhere isn't going anywhere."[25]

Somerville called the failure of churches to prioritize missions "majoring on the minors." Because so many churches "major on the minors," the world suffers. He even contended that the contemporary church (of the 1950s) was largely responsible for the contemporary chaos in the world. When churches are consumed with measuring their magnitude by materialism and when preachers are preoccupied with possessions like luxury clothes and cars, the church fails to fulfill its mission. He further insisted: "If we had loaned our sons to God as missionaries and ambassadors of goodwill, we would not be sending them as cannon's fodder on bloody Korean battlefields."[26]

In a frontal attack on churches that focused inwardly on what he frequently termed, the work of the church, he affirmed: "The great compassion of Jesus Christ is too big to be contained by us little people in our churches." He further raised a severe critique: "Is it true that many of our present-day Christians have erected magnificent churches and cathedrals to simply make them some sanctified Mausoleums where they have buried the Good News within the four walls of their sanctuary that they may 'enjoy' their religion in peace, comfort and serenity? Yes, the Good News has been embalmed with such thoroughness that its mummified corpse has become a valley of dry bones."[27]

Somerville lamented in a 1945 sermon: "Christ seems to be absent today in our churches." He detailed how, "We have our robed choirs. We have our newly renovated buildings. We have our well-trained preachers. We have our big bank accounts, ever buying war bonds with our surplus, and making money off the war. Don't we feel loneliness, coolness? Something seems to be missing."[28] This sentiment is a recurring theme over Somerville's decades of preaching and promoting the prioritization of missions in the life of the church. He bemoaned the fact that so many churches expended so much energy on "church work" rather than "the work of the church." "Church work" distracted attention and depleted energy for the life-giving work to which the church is called.

Individuals were called to repentance of their patterns of life as well. "While the hungry starve, the needy cry, injustice wanders at large, and the poor are sold for a pair of old shoes, we slumber on Beauty Rest® mattresses. Our super freezers provide our fresh foods in season and out of season. Our wardrobes bulge with expensive clothing for moth to feed upon."[29] Somerville was blistering in his attack on the self-centeredness expressed by so many Christians. The personal self-absorption of Christian people fueled the egocentric practices of many churches. He saw a critical need for refocusing energy and attention on the will of God in Jesus Christ to which all disciples were called—that the world might be saved in all the ways that humans need salvation.

Faithfulness to the life and work of Jesus means the church cannot be conformed to the patterns of the world. The church must challenge and transform the world. This approach to missional living, however, is demanding and threatening to the cultural status quo. "When Jesus led the protest against the selling of sacrificial animals in the outer court of the temple, and drove out the money changers, he appeared to be a dangerous leader of popular discontent…. Whenever the Christian church challenges the economic moguls, trouble begins."

Many Christians have sought a religious experience that affirms their versions for lives of social status, material increase, and luxurious living. Somerville's theology stands in stark contrast and direct opposition. He did not glorify poverty. However, he held that a comfortable Christian seemed an oxymoron. His understanding of faithful Christian living, both personally and in community, required one to invest one's life looking to the well-being of others as well as the well being of oneself. Further, one's own good fortune was intended to be used in the service of making the world a better place for those living most vulnerably at the margins. "The supreme tragedy of our times is the fact that the Christian message which started out as the most disturbing force ever to confront civilization, has today become one of the most soothing and complacent ways of life. … It is obvious that our religion has become too tranquil, cozy, relaxed, and untroubled. Well, let me remind you that if your religion does not have the potency to disturb you it doesn't have the strength to save you."[30] In a simultaneously humorous, yet serious anecdote, Somerville tells of a "certain preacher" who said he did not want Somerville to preach at his church. The rationale for not inviting Somerville to preach was that he would disturb the preacher's people, and the preacher did not want anyone to disturb his people.[31]

Somerville celebrated the disturbing capacity of the Gospel. He called for disturbing world leaders in global politics. The mandates of the Gospel offered clear alternatives to the execution of wars. He called for disturbance of the self-centered utilization of wealth in the United States to transform its preoccupation with accumulation toward a commitment to fair utilization of resources for the billions of poor people around the world. He argued, however, that "all of the fault cannot be placed upon the political and business leaders. The fault lies principally at the door of our churches." Further, he called for disturbing churches with revival in which Christians intentionally reach out to "sinners" who need to encounter the saving grace of God through Jesus Christ. "As I travel throughout this country, I find hundreds of churches tearing down their old barns and working overtime erecting palatial new barns to store their surplus corn. I am afraid that before they are able to completely relax from the efforts they put forth to build these new barns to store their surplus corn, the Angel may appear and say thou foolish one, this night thy soul is required to meet the Judge of all the earth, and then whose corn will it be?"[32] This corrective word to the 20th Century church of Somerville's era will continue to grow in relevance through the 21st Century as the disparity between the rich and the poor expands in the world generally, and in the church particularly.

Somerville lamented the materialization that charac-terized many of the churches he knew during his more than half century as a missional leader. He believed the warning attributed to Walter Rauschenbusch should be headed: "If the church does not succeed in Christianizing commerce, commerce will commercialize the church."[33]

Inspiration from Youth for the Church

Somerville believed the church was to be engaged substantially in the world for Christ. The biblical witness demanded this, and his missional experience and theological perspective sharply framed this principle. Somerville tells of how he once was amazed to happen upon a group of 150 hippies during a visit to India in the early 1960s who styled themselves as "The Love Generation" or "Flower Children".[34] He noticed banners they displayed that urged, "Burn pot, not people" and "Make love, not war." He further learned what he described as "a strange way of life" that claimed: "Do your own thing, but don't try to put your thing on anybody else." In conversation with some of these hippies, he concluded that they were actually in search of community and affirmation that they did not experience at their homes in the United States.

Upon discovering that Somerville was a preacher, one of the apparent leaders of this community said, "Preacher, why don't you come on the 'outside' of the church where the action is, and dig it?" Although he never understood what it meant to "dig it," Somerville discerned a connection that these young people had with a principle that is consistent with his understanding of the life and work of Jesus. Jesus, Somerville asserted, only preached one sermon "inside" his "home church" in Nazareth, and that sermon had power to transform the outside (ref. Luke 4:18-19).

Getting outside of the church to "where the action is" rests at the heart of Somerville's understanding of the church. He repeatedly criticized churches that were more committed to routine issues of maintenance than robust investments in missions. He further spoke often of "a little church within the church." This "church within the church" consisted of those who had been embraced by God's mission of redemption to the world. They understood that they were called to partner with Christ in bringing people to him so that they might encounter his transforming power and join him in bringing others to God through Christ. In a reference credited to Emil Brunner, Somerville believed "the church exists by missions as fire exists by burning."[35]

Somerville saw youth movements of the 1960s as a challenge to the church that should not be dismissed. He observed a search for meaning and a spiritual creativity that called the church to accountability. He also discerned an invitation to engagement and nurture. The outrage of youth toward what previous generations had done (e.g., wars, racism, exploitation of the weak, and the like) and an idealism to love and be loved personally and collectively were two sides of a complex reality. Youth were seeking to fill a spiritual vacuum.

He believed youth could see the hypocrisy of many churches as they focused on maintenance activity rather than missional action. Youth saw much irrelevance in the church, and that extraneous commotion was incapable of capturing their imaginations and energies. "The youth of today," he claimed, "can see the hypocrisy of many of our so-called churches as they major through circles, clubs, auxiliaries, anniversaries, and numerous other irrelevant toils. And they can clearly see the difference between doing church work and the work of the church." He chastised the "many parents, church leaders, and persons who represent the Geritol clan, who are continuing to live in the past and feel that all is lost and it is just a matter of time before the end will come. Well to those chronic doubters, skeptics and distrustful pessimists, I seem to discern the voice of the Eternal as He spoke to the youthful Samuel …" The almost 70-year-old Somerville was inspired by "a religious ferment of vast proportions seething on America's college campuses, on the beaches where there is a period of spiritual creativity without parallel in recent times; and, many are saying as Samuel spoke, 'Speak, Lord, for thy servant is listening.'"[36]

A Leadership Crisis

Somerville believed the contemporary church of his day lived in the tension of longing for a nostalgic past and striving for a relevant present. In the midst of this struggle, he was concerned about the quality of the leadership for and the witness of the church. He held that there were two particular pressures on the church of the 1960s. On one hand was a temptation to withdraw behind a fortress of tradition in fear of the complex changes of the day. Many people talked about "the good old days." On the other hand was the temptation to be drawn into the "main stream" of the world in the name of relevance. These Christians and their leaders turned to a relativism and revisionism of morality that resulted in Christian morality dissolving into a melting pot like everything else in the U.S. during that time.

Some wanted the church not to surrender her distinctive positions, while others wanted the church to catch up with the modern revolutions of the world. While every generation faces the tension of holding on to the past, embracing the present, and preparing for the future, Somerville saw a particular volatility in the 1960s that posed a unique challenge for the church. The "dynamic middle" that he called for was a deep loyalty to the gospel and a simultaneous sensitivity to the unique needs of "our troubled age." He urged reliance on the Holy Spirit—"the divine contemporary that remains the key to Christian living in this, as in all the past generations." Reliance on the Spirit would enable the church and its leaders to be true to the best of its foundations and competent to offer a credible witness in an age of swift transition.[37]

The Christian leader carries a substantial responsibility for his or her own service, as well as the example of service to the church and community. Missionally unfocused leadership in the church aggravated Somerville's through-out his missional career. For him, missional service was "the divine assignment." Christian missions, the main work of the church, was not something "taken up" by people. Christian missions was assigned by Jesus Christ to his immediate disciples and to all those who would believe throughout history. Avoidance of this divine assignment resulted in the anemic Christian witness of many churches of his day. Further, God's call to Christians for the work of missions is an act of grace. When one discerns this call to service, one does not work one's way up the ladder, but Jesus comes down the ladder to meet our needs and invite us to his service.[38]

In an intriguing sermon entitled, "When Leaders Go Fishing," Somerville turned to John 21 to highlight some of the tragic results when Christian leaders turn to fishing—preoccupying themselves with making a living, engaging in distractions to pass the time away, and turning to activities designed to help them forget their problems. These are terribly misdirected uses of time for those who have been given a divine assignment to take the gospel into the entire world. This weak and wayward leadership leads churches to fail in their missional mandates for the world.

Somerville believed that leaders set the tone for their communities. The oral tradition of the Lott Carey Convention reports that he frequently offered the following insight. "You can take a big preacher, put him in a little church, give him a little time, and he will bring the church up to his size. On the other hand, you can take a little preacher, put him in a great big church, give him a little time, and he will whittle the thing down to his size."

When leaders fail to commit themselves fully to the mission of Christ, congregations are not likely to commit themselves fully. He held that the evidence of leadership was seen in the missional commitment of the local church. "As a general rule, however, I have found that the spiritual temperature of any church can be determined by what it does 'for others,' and the leader creates that temperature. The size of the church, Christ within the church, is determined by the size of the preacher."[39]

Preoccupation with personal privilege and excess causes leaders to pursue paths of self-destruction and personal implosion. "Selfishness has often retarded God's plan, but selfishness will never stop it. Even some Christian leaders have joined the 'unauthorized sit down strike' against the onward march of the Gospel. Sometimes, God gets tired of our selfishness and will discharge us. Have you ever seen a discharged preacher? Everything he touches fails."[40] Failure of leaders to respond to the missional mandate of Christ yields devastating outcomes.

Public Witness and Prophetic Gospel

Wendell Somerville urged the church to call to accountability the social structures that oppose the principles of Christian communities. This call to prophetic witness was particularly needed in an age of militarism and materialism in the United States. "The real church does not consist of a host of sick saints and officials suffering with a chronic case of tired blood who gather on the Sabbath Day seeking to get a shot of tranquilizers to get them through the rest of the week. But it lies in the consciousness of its relationship with the big and universal issues on the outside of the four walls of our modern, well-appointed edifices."[41]

He rejected the notion that Christian faith could be privatized. While the commitment of life to God through Jesus Christ was personal, it was simultaneously communal and called for public practice. This public practice included the conviction that Christian people and the Christian church were obligated to participate in public discourse and engagement so that the Gospel could influence the lives of people at all levels of life.

Somerville lived during an era that witnessed the most dramatic changes of any comparable time period in history. "Since the beginning of the century the automobile has given [us] a pair of legs that can run over the highway at 130 miles per hour. The airplane has given [us] wings to fly faster than sound. The television has given [us] eyes and ears of a god. The atomic bomb has given [us] fists big enough and strong enough to kill a whole population at one blow. And as the satellites and missiles zoom over our heads, we ask, 'what next?'"[42] The rapid changes in technology, culture, economics, international relations, and the like were unprecedented. Somerville recognized the need for the church to work at being relevant in each age. Consequently, he frequently urged "that the church must reassess its role and responsibility in the world.... In facing our troubles, in this new day, the church must get a greater clarity, urgency and relevance of what Christ has assigned the church to do in the world."[43]

Somerville's commitment to "foreign missions" did not preclude him from speaking to the domestic challenges in the United States. He forcefully and insightfully interpreted social challenges through the lenses of the Gospel in numerous sermons. He called Christians to follow Christ's commitment to the poor, sick, and defenseless in every way. He was an advocate on behalf of the vulnerable and was repulsed by the manipulation of political, economic, and social systems by the strong to the detriment of the weak. He was appalled by the excessive expenditures by the U.S. government on "massive killing machines" when, in his view, so much more good would result from investing in the things that improved the quality of life for the massive numbers of poor people in the U.S. and around the world. He was bewildered that such massive amounts of funds could be invested in space exploration while programs designed to enable people to strengthen themselves, their families, and their communities received pittances in comparison. Somerville believed the narratives that communicate the deep compassion of Jesus for people who suffer call Christians to reassess their understanding of faith.

Taking a cue from the biblical witness of Esther, Somerville contended that neither the church nor the nation could afford to keep silent in the face of the local, national, and global pain and destruction of the 1950s. Perhaps, he held, salvation would come from Communism, Islam, or nationalism should the Christian church renege on its obligation to be agents of God's salvation. Further, despite the hardships of slavery, segregation, and discrimination on the Negro Church of his day, Somerville argued that the formerly insignificant Esther was brought to a prominent place of influence for a critical time. Likewise, the American Negro Christian, though thought insignificant by much of the dominant culture, should not believe it would escape a destruction that could come on the United States because of its failed moral and spiritual condition. The Negro Church could not remain silent. It had people of influence and purpose given to it by God.[44] What was true of the Negro Church that Somerville knew best was, likewise, true for the church irrespective of ethnic composition.

The church of the 1950s and 1960s, Somerville believed, "has found herself in a peculiar situation." The church's curious predicament was its challenge to negotiate multiple voices and messages in response to war and to find its proper posture. First, there was the voice coming from the church that "simply echoed every word which has been handed to the preacher from the minister of propaganda." The church had been used as a marketplace for selling war bonds, perpetuating Jim Crow laws for discrimination, and the like. "It has given its full support to the killing business."

Second, there was the voice of expediency and safety that gave verbal affirmation for and support to "the war makers." However, the church that used its voice like this felt condemnation and shame within its soul because of the "bloody business of war." Third, there was a voice that "constantly and consistently contended that war and murder are never justified in the light of the teachings of the Prince of Peace. This voice has continued to say that love is greater than hate. That reason is better than war. And that right is greater than might."[45]

Somerville was a vigorous critic of Christians who chose complacency over missional engagement. Lethargy concerning societal ills resulted in tragic consequences hurtful to those who lived most vulnerable to exploitation from imbalances of power. The disengagement of the faithful made the way for fearful consequences for marginalized communities. Shortly after the gubernatorial elections of two segregationists, Somerville named the dire consequences of Christian complacency for the political process in the nation. "The recent primary election in Maryland where the racial bigot George P. Mahoney and in Georgia where the arch segregationist Lester Maddox were nominated for Governors came because the so-called Christians complacently sat in their comfortable pews in their Gothic Cathedrals listening to solemn music as these false prophets, preachers, and church officers with tired-blood sang 'whiter than snow, yes whiter than snow Lord, wash me and I shall be whiter than snow'. That is white power personified." Somerville believed Christians were obligated to move beyond the comforts of church campuses and engage the world with the Gospel of Jesus Christ. This meant challenging poverty, war, and oppression, as well as seeking those who were lost in sin.[46]

Too much was believed to be at stake for those with the fewest resources to survive, not to mention thrive, for Christians to fail to assert themselves appropriately for good. "Despite the fact I have spent the last 40 years working among the teeming millions of hungry, diseased, and ignorant people throughout the world," Somerville declared in a 1980s-era sermon, "I know that poverty is not a necessity, but an evil, an injustice, and an offense against mankind, wherever it exists. ... Remember, we have not preached a full salvation until we have offered the teeming millions some hope of a successful escape from poverty, hunger, disease, and ignorance."[47]

Somerville concluded that the church could offer no valid excuse for its failure to engage the world in robust missional ways. Failure to do so made the church complicit in creating unreasonable suffering for the most vulnerable people in the world. "The Christian church stands condemned in its concern for people. Christ taught that we should treat other people exactly as we would like to be treated by them. Ours is an affluent society in which the few have too much and the many have too little. ...Remember, the Kingdom of God belongs to the man who humbly rests his poverty in God's wealth, his ignorance in God's wisdom, his sin in God's mercy, his moral failures and his battle with his temptations in God's grace."[48]

Somerville vigorously attacked attitudes that enabled the church to enjoy privilege at the expense of the impoverished.

The average Christian has so accustomed himself to a life of ease, complacency, contentment, and satisfaction, that he is totally blind and ignorant to the essential meaning of what it means to actually follow Jesus. I have not come today with an idea of bringing soothing syrup or to dilly dally with this vital matter, but I have come to challenge the devil and his hosts on this subject of Right and Wrong. … To share with the crushed, neglected, exploited, and broken fragments of humanity today is an unpopular course to take. In the alleys and slums of our city are numerous souls waiting for you to lift them up. They are there for no fault of their own, but are the victims of a vicious system."[49]

Somerville understood the basis for conflict in the world was tension between those that have excess and those that do not have enough. These extremes created discord all over the world.[50] This dissonance was capable of producing tragic, even fatal, consequences.

War and Christian Witness

"[A]ll war," according to Somerville, "is contrary to the teachings of Jesus."[51] More than three and one-half decades following the preceding statement, he was amazingly consistent as he wrote: "Certainly our national leaders are unaware that war is incompatible with the doctrines of Christ."[52] The tragedies of the U.S. bombings of Hiroshima and Nagasaki stood out prominently in his mind, and the U.S. acceleration to greater and greater capacity for military annihilation distressed him. He concluded that atomic energy and spiritual power were the two most potent forces existent in the 1940s. Regrettably, and perhaps unforgivably, proponents of atomic energy were progressing rapidly in expanding their capability for destruction while Christians were not aggressively advancing the Gospel appropriate to the urgency of the day.

There were already enough bombs to destroy the earth. Somerville wondered why there was need for more. The Christian Church should have been driven by the urgent need of the majority of people in the world to hear the Gospel. He believed people would be saved in proportion to the evangelistic intentionality of the church. The church should not have been paralyzed by fear. In his mind, the lack of urgency expressed by much of Christianity contributed substantially to the problem of the nation's preoccupation with war. In a stinging 1947 indictment, Somerville wrote: "It may be the cause of this international insanity can be traced to the church itself."[53]

As a global missions leader, Somerville consistently viewed U.S. war policies negatively. It appeared to him that there was a disproportionate investment in weaponry as compared to support that would address the problems of poverty and oppression of people around the world. His insight of 1976 is representative of his consistent posture regarding war, whether World War II, Korea, Vietnam, or the varieties of military intervention or support given by the U.S. government around the world.

> Our whole world today is engulfed in a mad scramble for greedy power through war, massive crime and evils of every description. Current records show that our own America sold nine billion dollars in guns (killing machines) to foreign countries last year, and at the same time we are screaming from the house-top that we are "seeking peace" in the Middle East, in Rhodesia and in South Africa. As I stood in Moscow last year and observed the current scene, I recalled the memorable words of the celebrated Russian Novelist who wrote in his classic novel in 1880—*War and Peace*—"when murder is elevated to become a virtue, all kinds of crime will flourish." Believe me; it would appear that this prophetic message is daily being unfolded not only in the non-Christian lands, but in our own great country.[54]

Somerville was distressed by the immense increases in military spending undertaken by the Reagan administration in the early 1980s. His disdain for the annihilating military actions in Japan during World War II resurfaced with his assessment that the U.S. government would produce nerve gas to obliterate the nervous systems of people for a 100-mile radius. He agreed with Admiral Noel Gayler, former director of the National Security Agency and commander of U.S. forces in the Pacific, that "there is no sensible military use of any of our nuclear forces, intercontinental theater or tactical." Against these life-threatening forces, Somerville lifted his commitment to the Christian message of salvation and redemption for all and the power available to those who believe in God.[55] He was an unapologetic advocate of the biblical teaching to love one's enemies and to overcome evil with good. Throughout his tenure as a missional leader, Somerville saw U.S. governmental policy fail to respond with ultimate wisdom again and again.

Somerville believed it a sign that the world had caught up with the church whenever the world approved of the church's work. When this happens, it is time for the church to take a step forward. He challenged the church of Jesus Christ to go beyond any contemporary national, political, or cultural divisions. The church could not, to his understanding, be loyal to its mission while identifying itself with any one group of people. "She sees more clearly than any statesman, politician, or religious racketeer. She is without any illusion and self-deception. The terrific danger ahead is for any compromising with the forces of evil." He saw compromise in examples such as Francis Cardinal Spellman and the evangelist Billy Graham praying for U.S. soldiers as they killed people in Vietnam. To Somerville, it was inconceivable that Christian leaders would "bless" the war efforts in Vietnam or any other expressions of massacre and destruction. His condemnation, however, was not of the soldiers faithfully executing their orders. His reproach was for the U.S. government that sent the soldiers to war and the Christian leaders and people who gave religious affirmation to the killing.[56]

Somerville struggled with the inconsistency of characterizing the killing of a civilian murder, while waging devastating war strategies that killed innocent people— particularly women and children—in Japan, Korea, and Vietnam. How could the U. S. government execute foreign policies like those that provided arms in Pakistan and then criticize India for not preventing war? The church could not be silent in the face of devastating international intervention. He argued, "Neither a nation nor an individual can start doing right until it stops doing wrong."[57] Because the church is committed to the principles of the community of God, it must be a witness to the powers of the world for God's way of peace and protection and provision for the vulnerable and the victimized. Somerville's dismay with the illogical preoccupation and interest in war is demonstrated in observations like this:

> Our tangled world needs a rebirth of faith and hope. …The United States government is spending $20 billion a year killing innocent people in Vietnam. In other words, the Pentagon admits that it cost the United States $332,000 for every Viet Cong we kill. Do you realize what this means?
>
> We spent more money last year for killing machines than all of the Christians have given for Christian missions since the day of Pentecost. … The Christian Church is on trial. We have got to arise and make all men believe that they are made in the image of God. Then they will develop a new concept of saneness, justice, and responsibility.[58]

Somerville consistently held that war could never bring equitable or lasting resolution to conflicts.

> One of the strange paradoxes of our generation is the fact that President Eisenhower asked the 86th Congress to give him forty billion dollars in order to buy some bigger and deadlier guns and bombs than Russia has. Congress gave him his appropriation. Now with all of these so-called killing machines, President Eisenhower is afraid to sit down at a conference table with Nikita Khrushchev, for he knows that guns can't save us. History has proven that a nation's only sure defense is an inner defense— to do justly, love mercy, and to walk humbly with God.[59]

Somerville was constantly baffled at the obsession of world leaders for war and destruction. Focusing on the immediate present at the expense of the distant future was leading to devastating decisions on a world-wide scale. In his mind, continual commitments to increase arsenals of conventional and nuclear weapons could only lead to further deaths of innocent civilians and youthful soldiers and, perhaps, to the destruction of the world as he knew it. He rejected the view that war was inevitable and that ever increasing military budgets were essential to guarantee the security of the nation. To the contrary, he saw the escalation of military capacities as threatening to security because the increases of war capabilities on one side inevitably provoked increases on the other side. Essentially, he believed "missiles are not symbols of strength, but they are signs of fear and weakness. A reliance on might is never enough to give a people security."[60] Christians should not be silent before or supportive of unrestrained military buildups. There was a clear decision that needed to be made by Christians. Choose missions or missiles.

Somerville was amazed that the political leaders of the era during the presidencies of Dwight D. Eisenhower and John F. Kennedy could not realize they had reached "the saturation point of overkill, and only mad men would want to continue rushing towards Armageddon." He further declared: "It has been left to us who acknowledge, love, and accept [Jesus Christ] to save [humanity] from annihilation. It is our task to challenge and condemn the present missile-minded world and to transform it. If we fail to accept our responsibility, the Eternal may have to make a new start with His original design for the earth and they that dwell therein."[61] Rather than enthusiastically embracing the use of weapons that caused devastation of churches, annihilation of homes, destruction of schools, demolition of hospitals, and obliteration of social institutions for the well being of communities and humanity, Christians should call world leaders to do justly, love mercy, and walk humbly with God.

Somerville's conviction about the incongruity of war and Christian witness was not only global and congregational. It applied to the personal level. Recruiting young people of Christian communities for world missions was a goal to which Somerville aspired for churches. In order for more congregations to send out their best and brightest young men and women in missions, families had to embrace this desire. Inspired by the witness of Hannah who promised God to return for service a son that she asked to be born (1 Samuel 1), Somerville believed the "current challenge of the Christian mothers of the USA is to offer their sons and daughters to God as Christian missionaries rather than allowing them to become common fodder." He believed the failure of the church to send more young men and women into Christian missions globally was directly related to the large numbers of young adults being sent by the government as fodder for war. "It will either be missions or missiles."[62]

The darkest day in human history for Somerville was August 6, 1945 when the U.S. dropped the atomic bomb on Hiroshima.[63] He held that this tragedy was related to racism. More blood was shed that day over "race" than for any other purpose in history. He further believed race was an artificial social construct, or as he articulated it, "a man made term." The horror inflicted on people by people over race is opposed to God's vision for humanity. While the problems of racism were of major importance to Somerville because of his theological understanding of God's concern and the church's obligation to the entire world, the dilemma of race was particularly problematic for Somerville because of his intense identification as a black American with Africa.

A Strategy for Africa and a Vision for the Black Church

Somerville took seriously the role of Lott Carey as an African American foreign missions agency among the collection of North American global missions organizations. The struggles black communities and individuals faced in the United States were acknowledged but not accepted as reason for non-engagement in missions around the world.

He was confident of God's hand upon them through their struggles and sure of God's call for them to engage the world for Christ.

> The hour has arrived for the Christians of America, especially the non-white Christians, to demonstrate to the world that the gospel message of Jesus Christ is sufficient to set an upset world right side up. The courage, patience, faith and fortitude of the nine children of Little Rock have awakened the conscience of peoples throughout the world.[64] Never in the history of a people has the hand of God been more plainly seen than it has within recent months. It is our responsibility to carry this courage, patience and faith in the Eternal God to the darker people throughout the world.[65]

Early in Wendell Somerville's career of leadership with Lott Carey, he promoted the unparalleled global scope of the African American organization. The global reach of the Lott Carey Convention was an outgrowth of its commitment to liberal distribution of God's resources among those in the world with less than enough. "Religion has value only as it is shared," Somerville declared. "Every penny received by the Lott Carey Convention comes from Negroes, yet we support white missionaries in Europe, black missionaries in Haiti and Africa, yellow men in China, and Brown men in India."[66]

In the 1940s, Somerville argued that God must have a special purpose in mind for Africa. Despite the exploitation and ravaging experienced by the people and the land, it remained intact. The question was, "Why has God kept Africa that great question mark for thousands of generations?" He contended that practically every European war had been fought over Africa, yet she still stood. Why? God has a purpose for Africa.

A critical issue for Somerville, given his assertion of the importance of Africa to God, was how the American Negro might cooperate with God to bring about the realization of God's plan for the continent. He saw a stupendous, yet dangerous, opportunity akin to the experience of Caleb and Joshua who asserted that Israel was able to seize the promise land, in contrast to the majority report from the reconnaissance team to the land of God's promise that cast Israel as grasshoppers in opposition to giants. Somerville's strategy follows.[67]

First, the American Negro community needed to prepare their best minds to go to Africa and offer leadership and support in a variety of areas. In spite of segregation, the American Negro enjoyed significant academic and economic opportunities in comparison to Africans. The Christian response, therefore, should be to send their most gifted sons and daughters to Africa for service in economic, industrial, educational, and spiritual areas as part of the global Christian witness.

Second, the American Negro Church needed to sacrifice significant sums of money to bring promising young Africans to the United States for higher education. This would give African youth exposure to the relatively higher quality of preparation available to their American counterparts. Somerville's argument was that other countries (e.g., China, Japan, India, etc.) invested in the education of their youth. Why could not American Negroes sacrifice some of their luxuries for this purpose?

Third, the American Negro Church needed to cultivate the cooperation of American whites who shared opposition to the exploitation of Africa. Negroes should not assume they were alone in their commitment to African people realizing their full spiritual, personal, communal, and national potential. Collaboration would be an important strategic component for the liberation of Africa and the obliteration of imperialism.

Failure to seize the opportunity for intentional engagement with Africa by the American Negro Christian community would bring serious consequences. Just as Israel suffered death and a 40-year delay of entering the land God had promised, the people to whom Somerville sought to challenge potentially faced a great cost for failing to accept this dangerous opportunity. Somerville asserted:

"If Christianity is to win in Africa we must send American Negro missionaries. The Negro church must eliminate its grasshopper church officers and heed the courageous call of Caleb—'Let us go up at once and possess the land for we are able to overcome it.'"[68]

Born in 1900, Somerville knew by experience and observation the heavy loads African Americans carried. The social crises that engulfed American cities, the problems of the ghettos, the intolerable conditions endured in rural areas, and the resistance against African American attempts to find better lives weighed heavily on him. This prompted him to think and to speak intentionally on the role of the American Negro Church and missions. In essence, he was interpreting and giving definition to what he and the Lott Carey organization had practiced for decades. He stated, "All my life I have been aware of the tremendous crosses which my ancestors and I have been forced to bear through the years. However, it has been within recent years, as I have traveled around the world, that I have discovered God's design in using us to serve as a symbol of his divine plan." He concluded that Negro Christians had a divine assignment to teach the technique of survival through faith, to be instruments through which God speaks, and to be a voice of humanity's last hope of redemption.[69]

Prior to the end of the 1960s, Somerville spoke of American Negro Christianity. By the end of the decade, he used the language "Black Church," indicating his attention to the burgeoning black theology/black church movement pioneered as a theological response to the black power movement in the country. Somerville, however, moved beyond a culturally convenient identification with a creative biblical hermeneutic that connected the growing consciousness within black theological circles and among some Black Church leadership of the era. "The origin of the Black Church," he asserted, "became evident on that memorable occasion as recorded in Mark's Gospel 15:21 where it is recorded, 'On their way out of the city they met a man called Simon, a native of Cyrene in Africa, and they compelled him to carry Jesus' Cross;' and, during the past 19 turbulent centuries this Black Church has preserved the Christian faith as enunciated by the Son of God."[70]

Wendell Somerville believed the Black Church was called to empower black people spiritually and socially. He believed it was called to engage in missions globally and holistically. He also believed that "just as God called Paul to be the missionary to the Gentiles, so He is today calling the black church to become the missionaries to the white man. Yes, the black church is called upon to spiritually empower black people, and at the same time to liberate white people from the shackles of institutional racism which is the basis of our present social cancer in our national and local civic and religious life."[71] This "divine assignment" was something given to the Black Church. It had not volunteered for its unique role. The role was given to it out of the eternal mind and will of God.

Somerville believed white racists had inherited their illness, and God had placed the vaccine in the hands of black people. He interpreted this responsibility in view of the cross in relationship to redemption and salvation. A pivotal point of biblical inspiration for him was Simon of Cyrene's being compelled to carry the cross of Jesus to the place of crucifixion. Simon became the only "friend" the Son of God had in bearing the cross, and bearing the cross made Simon a participant in God's atoning work through the death of Jesus. "The more I study this tragic scene," Somerville declared, "the more I can understand the role that the black man has been called upon to perform in establishing the Cross as the center of mankind's redemption and salvation."[72]

Somerville believed black Christians must think black, but act colorlessly. While acknowledging the apparent contradiction of this methodology to some, he nonetheless argued for the interrelatedness of particularity and universality. He pointed to the fact that Jesus was born, lived, and died a Jew. However, his actions were not limited by the distinctiveness of his ethnicity. Additionally, the Holy Spirit converted the racism of Simon Peter as noted in

Acts 10-11. Neither Jesus, Peter, nor Paul ever stopped being Jews. Their actions, however, were not constricted by their ethnicity. Somerville believed this to be the logic of the work of Martin Luther King, Jr. King was born, lived, and died black, but his life's commitment to nonviolent strategies to win equality for all people went beyond his blackness. To further make his point, Somerville pointed to Japan. Although pulverized by atomic bombs, Japan continued to "think Brown." As a result, Japan thrived and was headed to become an economic and political leader in the world.[73]

Black Christians should not deny their blackness, but their missional activity should not be limited by it. There was no reason for blacks to abandon their churches for white churches. He recognized that many black people who left black institutions for white ones were denying their cultural identities. He lamented that they would sometimes succumb to strategies of white congregations and institutions to compromise them by giving their new black participants and congregants positions of perceived power, but no real authority. By thinking black and acting colorlessly, black Christians fully measure up to the standards of Christ and become extraordinary Christians. In Somerville's thought, this is love.

By thinking black and acting colorlessly, the Black Church continues to bring hope and inspiration to black people. The institutional and personal racism with which black Americans have struggled is discouraging and dehumanizing. The Black Church, by thinking black and acting colorlessly, has the capacity to empower and equip black people to both survive and thrive. Further, thinking black and acting colorlessly enables the Black Church to engage effectively in global missions. While black Christians should collaborate with white Christians for the cause of Christ, the global experiences of white imperialism and exploitation hinder the impact of missions by white missionaries and their agencies. The doors to a more effective Christian witness around the world are open to the Black Church because black people share experiences of oppression with the majority of people around the world.

Hindrances to the Black Church on Mission

Wendell Somerville had a robust missional vision for the Black Church. There were tremendous obligations and opportunities to live into its "divine assignment." If it was faithful, it would enjoy the privilege of laboring with Christ in redeeming the world to God. Somerville was not romantic, however, about the realities that hindered the successful execution of the missional agenda of the Black Church. Poor leadership and self-centeredness that inflicted many churches in many ethnic communities infected the Black Church of Somerville's era as well. There was much to rejoice about in the Black Church. There also was much cause for dismay and disgust.

Cutting at the culture of many African American churches of his era, Somerville criticized the conducting of "so-called revivals" that were ingrained in the customs of the churches he knew. He claimed that, too often, revivals were mechanisms to raise money, as opposed to ministries to empower people to further missional work. He disapproved of the extravagant planning and execution of various anniversaries that celebrated people rather than advancing the purposes of Christ. He denounced the limitless organizations and auxiliaries that churches put in place that served more for entertainment and social status.[74] Somerville seemed to grow more frustrated with the focus on non-essential activities that comprised "church work" which siphoned personal and fiscal resources that should have been concentrated on "the work of the church."

Somerville was especially severe in his critique of poor pastoral leadership in the Black Church.

> I know of no single sentence that is more pertinent as it relates to the average Negro church than this message ["And they did not for a single day stop teaching and preaching in the temple and in private houses the good news of Jesus Christ" (Acts 5:42)]. The average Negro Baptist preacher has become so intoxicated with his own self-importance and grandeur that he spends the major portion of his

time exalting and proclaiming himself as the center of attraction. A study of the average Negro church will show that it has called a moratorium on the task of 'going into the entire world,' and has stopped altogether in the world missionary endeavor.

Some have descended to such a low estate that they have taken the funds that the people have contributed for missions and have used these funds for local current expenses. The current *Unpardonable Sin* [emphasis in the original] is for a minister to allow his congregation to do more for him than he has led these same people to do for others.[75]

The church is called to both proclaim and perform the gospel. Somerville believed the Black Church had a great record of proclaiming the gospel, but it had been "miserly" in performing the gospel. "The church that is Big in proclaiming and Little in performing," he declared, "is like the train whose whistle was so big and required so much steam to blow it, that whenever the whistle would blow the train would stop."[76] Somerville did not believe the church should minimize proclamation. Instead, the church should put greater emphasis on the performance—doing the gospel. The world, he was convinced, waits for Christians who will both speak and serve.

The Missional Life

Given the tremendous resources in the available to people in the United States, Wendell Clay Somerville consistently called for a greater spirit of sacrifice. Living in the wealthiest nation in the world, he perceived the unlimited opportunities for investment that could benefit those who suffered and struggled most. The greater one's opportunities, he believed, the greater one's responsibilities.[1] Fulfilling the great missional possibilities for Christians, however, is beyond the capacity to attain alone. Jesus Christ leads disciples into full missional living.

The incarnation that the world sees in Jesus is the method of missions that Christians and churches should embrace. "The method of Jesus was to go where [one] was and then save [him or her]."[2] The missional task of Christians, therefore, is to go wherever people are and to lead them toward where they can be. Christ did not save people because of who they were. He saved people because of love. Consequently, new possibilities for what they were capable of becoming opened.

How sad it is that so few churches emulate the missional model of Christ. "Too many churches are trying to confine Jesus to their little narrow four walls. Your walls are not high enough to contain him. They are too thin to confine him. If we would join him as the Seeker and Savior of mankind, we must move outside the four walls of our comfortable churches, out in the open, out on the frontiers, and make our abodes in tents."[3] Consequently, he believed there was no need to get more people into conventional churches. The need was to get more of God in people. This would lead people to follow the pattern of Jesus who never asked where one came from but only wanted to know where one was going.

Global Vision

Somerville held "the central aim of foreign missions is to *make the Lord Jesus Christ* known to *all* [people] *everywhere* and to persuade them to accept Him as their Lord and master" (emphasis in the original)[4]. The urgency of this task was essentially two-fold. First was what he called "the Divine Assignment," which referred to Jesus' commissioning of his disciples and those who would follow him in successive generations to be his witnesses in word and deed. Second, the missional task throughout the world was urgent to him because in every generation troubled people all around the globe desperately ask "Is there any word from the Lord?"

Foreign missions, however, faced substantial opposition throughout the world. Those that carry the gospel globally are constantly contending against principalities, powers, rulers of present darkness, and spiritual wickedness. Somerville saw opposition to Christian missions in communism, oppressive non-Christian religions, nationalism, commercialism, moral and ethical decay, war, and the failure of churches to recruit young people for missions candidacy.[5]

Bringing people to know Christ required partnership, according to Somerville. While God has the power to save every human life, God partners with people to reach the world. This is a privilege, and it calls for a response of cooperation with God's plan of redemption for the world. This partnership of humanity with God for redeeming the world also requires a partnership with the global Christian community. Local churches must cultivate visions that extend beyond their own immediate horizons. Just as Jesus envisioned his call to the world, Christians in each era must embrace a vision to reach the world for Christ. "The current population explosion does not mean a decrease in our missionary effort; rather it means an increase in our responsibilities. The present increase in the world population is taking place among the least able to support themselves."[6]

God's mission to the world is global. Somerville believed the world suffered a great tragedy as "little-minded" people sought to localize the reach that Jesus intended for the world. People who seek to restrict the work of Christ to their localities fail to comprehend the scope and scale of Christ's mission. Christ cannot be circumscribed to any one segment of one's world. God's reach transcends all boundaries— racial, geographical, social, and the like. God's concern is for all, and consequently, those who follow Christ must invest their lives in others throughout the world.[7]

The Significance of Jesus Christ

Somerville was a realist about the bleak condition of the 20th Century. He spoke of "a cloud of darkness which enshrouds the universe," and lamented how much of the world, including his own U.S.A., was "undergoing a moral and spiritual blackout." He knew war, exploitation, discrimination, disparity between the wealthy and impoverished, disintegrating morality, and the like. He found poverty in the midst of plenty, affliction in the midst of affluence, and injustice in the midst of claims to righteousness. He held, however, that the apparent hopelessness of his world was nothing new. "Approximately 55 years after the death of Christ, a similar darkness engulfed mankind. Paul had been beheaded. Peter had been crucified. The temple had been burned by Titus, and thousands of early Christians were being thrown to wild beast while others were burned." The first century church was engaged in a battle between good and evil, and no subsequent generation has been free from the struggle between light and darkness.

In spite of the desperation of the ancient and contemporary worlds caused by sin, Somerville confidently proclaimed, "human nature can be changed, redeemed, transformed, and lifted up to new heights of devotion, loyalty, and sacrifice when the Light of Jesus Christ enters in and takes possession." He further declared that, "Jesus stands in the center of history. He has brought God and [humanity] into a new relationship and there is still more to be learned for those who seek diligently to discover who Jesus really is."[8]

He grieved at how many churches had succumbed to self-centeredness. They would often invest in themselves rather than feed the hungry, heal the sick, and bring the lost to relationship in Christ. Some churches, he conceded, were failing to live up to the standards and teachings of Jesus. Consequently, many people were leaving the church in disgust. However, Somerville claimed that the apparent darkness in which many churches were living was not due to the fact that the light of Christ had gone out in the church. Instead, he claimed an eclipse was being witnessed.

The light of Christ had not been extinguished. People were experiencing a temporary and partial hiding of the sun. He held the confident position that the light of Christ remained ablaze. Although it did look bleak for the church, he advanced the gospel found in John that "The light is still shining in the darkness, for the darkness has never put it out" (John 1:5). He illustrated his conviction through the following story.

> The minister of a little church in Europe got an electrician to put a cross on top of the church building that would light up at night. When the war came, bombs fell on the city and all the lights in the town went out. Although the lights inside the church went out, the lighted cross atop the building strangely remained lighted. The people sought out the electrician to inquire why all the other lights in the city had gone out but the light on the cross atop the building continued to shine. The electrician replied, "Well, I put in a secret cable which ran directly to the big dynamo at the power house." When the church maintains a direct connection to the Power House—God—our lights will never fail![9]

God reveals God's purposes and power fully in Jesus. "Jesus is the window through which we see as much of God as [humanity] is capable of beholding." Further, Christians partner with Christ in his work of redemption.[10]

The incarnational character of Christian missions grows out of the incarnation of Jesus whose life was largely spent among common people and suffering people. Consequently, Jesus understood deeply and intimately the realities of those who struggled from day to day. This understanding of the life and work of Jesus informed Somerville's missional commitment that Christians must work humbly and authentically among ordinary people, as well as among those who suffer and struggle. Somerville believed "all you have to do is to trace to its source any universal manifestation of human concern for the poor, afflicted, suffering, down-trodden, and oppressed, and you will discover a band of Christians may be doing the work of the church—not just doing church work."[11]

Somerville recognized an inseparable bond between his understanding of Christology and missions. For him, "the life, teaching, suffering, death, and resurrection of Jesus Christ all had one distinct meaning, and that meaning was that *all* men might be saved."[12] He understood Jesus' priority to search for and to save the lost. Further, he took seriously the biblical teaching of Jesus having "sheep that are not of this fold." His application of this concept was that a global (or as he would often say, universal) reach of missions and evangelism was required. This understanding of Christ drove his global commitment for evangelism to all ethnic groups.

Somerville drew a powerful illustration of his understanding of the universality of Christ's appeal. A little Chinese girl gave the testimony that "I have known him all my life, and one day I learned his name."[13] The above quote is consistent with other claims where Somerville appears to believe that an evangelist should not assume the absence of God when arriving in "unchurched" areas of the world. Some have argued that their tasks have been to bring God to people in various lands. Somerville's approach seems wide enough to conclude that the role of the missionary evangelist may be to bring the revelation of Jesus Christ as the Son of the Living God rather than to assume that one must bring God into an otherwise God-less context. These are radically different approaches that impact the respect for humanity and the humility with which many approach so-called foreign cultures.

Somerville interpreted Jesus' commissioning of his disciples to go into all of the world to make disciples, baptize them, and teach them, to be emphasizing "the conviction that He stands before His, and our, generation with a commission of His own from God that has no counterpart in the past, the present, nor the future. There is an aggressiveness about Jesus and a radical seriousness about His challenge that differentiated Him from all others. Therefore, His great commission brings a vertical vision to bear upon every horizontal situation."[14]

Somerville believed in the relevance of the Christian gospel in every generation. The Christian message "is as relevant today as this morning's sunrise."[15] This message is both a critique and a corrective for the false answers of the world for meaning and progress. The world he inhabited was misguided by the allures of military power and an assumption of security through wealth. The excessive military budgets and aggression of the United States in Vietnam resulted in unnecessary death and destruction. The extreme wealth of the country in comparison to most countries around the world did not prevent excesses of substance abuse and addiction, crime, and sinful lifestyles. As far as he was concerned, the false allures of the world had amply demonstrated their insufficiencies, and the Gospel of Jesus Christ offered the only true hope for the world.

Christ impacts our understanding of humanity. Somerville believed we should never underestimate the value of people. Regardless of their socio-economic conditions, cultures, or religious heritage, people are valued by God. Consequently, people should value each other. This world view results from a life of following Jesus.

When people know Christ, Somerville believed, they develop a sympathetic understanding of the problems of other people. Misunderstanding, in his mind, was crucial to many personal and national conflicts. Further, knowing Christ has healing power for physical and mental ailments. In addition, knowing Christ leads one to overcome barriers that have been erected by traditions and cultural contexts. Knowing Christ also enables one to discern one's personal inadequacies and to recognize the power of Christ to transform them. Beyond this, knowing Christ leads people to share joyfully their blessings with others, and their unselfish service is rewarded. People who know Christ do not ask, "What's the payoff?" However, God has a way of rewarding those who share what they have received.[16]

Being free in Christ gives one a sense of dignity, and dignity is as essential to the human condition as food and shelter. When Christians live missionally, they can bring people to saving relationships in Christ, and this empowers people to strive for dignity in their lives and in the lives of others. During the U.S. Civil Rights Movement, Somerville understood the demands of Christian living to embrace traditional evangelical efforts of leading people to life commitments to Jesus, and an outgrowth of this life was to work for the freedom of oppressed people from racial injustice. Freedom, he argued, was not something that simply fell upon people. To the contrary, people had to rise up to freedom. "Freedom does not descend upon a people. They must rise up to it. Freedom is like the green substance in the plant—photosynthesis."[17] The Spirit of Christ within people moved them to rise up to seize and secure the freedom God intended for them. The freedom one finds in Christ, Somerville's logic holds, drives one to seek the freedom of other people. Abiding in Christ leads disciples to this kind of freedom-seeking living.[18]

Salvation

Those who meet Christ discover the global reach of God's mission. "There are many people who want to circumscribe

Christ into some little local church, family, or denominational enclosure. ... The records show that wherever he went he carried a universal message of salvation to everyone who would believe and accept God's free gift of salvation."[19]

Somerville lamented attempts by people to separate the human family on the bases of color, race, physical attributes, and the like. He had a robust view of the human family as being the sheep of God who are not of "this" fold, in reference to Jesus' words recorded in John 10:16. While his theology was unapologetically Christocentric, he still embraced a vision of God's inclusivity that supersedes human categorization and exclusivity. In his own preaching voice, Somerville would declare: "Let us take a glance at those other sheep that are not of our fold: 217 million Hindus, 12 million Jews, 260 million Confucianists, 300 million Muslims, 650 million Communists, and ½ billion others who have never known or heard of the Good Shepherd."[20]

Somerville's understanding of the transforming power of Christ is illustrated in the following story he would tell in sermons.

> Two men were discussing the miracle where Christ changed water into wine. One said, "You think that is something. I saw him turn liqueur into milk."
>
> "How?" inquired the other.
>
> "Well, until four years ago I drank so much hard liqueur that people believed that I was embalmed with hard liqueur. I heard an old ignorant preacher talk about Jesus. I took him at his word. This Christ transformed my life. The money that I put into liqueur is now used to purchase milk for my five children."[21]

Somerville believed all human beings possess a "dim inner light"—a mysterious essence that is a gift from God. An authentic encounter with Christ, or "finding Christ" as he would say, ignites this "dim flicker" and opens people to the inspiration of God in their lives. This leads people toward the missional work of Christ that glorifies God and benefits humanity.[22] "What we need today," he claimed, "is not more religion. We need to use more of the religion we already have. [One] must remember that the things that are really our aim are not the things we possess, but the thing that possess us."[23] At another time he declared, "What we need is not more [people] in the church, but we need more church in the [people] we have."[24]

One seeks to understand the needs of people when one encounters Christ. For Somerville, finding Christ produces the will and capacity to understand the needs of people. Disciples of Christ seek to appreciate and address the complexity of human needs. Interest in the well being of others is not just for their spiritual security or for the salvation of the soul alone. Human needs include food, clothing, the desire to belong, security, and the like. Faith that has nothing to do with human suffering has nothing to do with God. Finding Christ leads one toward holistic interest and investment in the lives of people around the world. People consist of components, divisions, fractures, and disconnections until they find Christ. One only finds one's true self in Christ.

Serving among those who suffer and struggle has salvific implications for missional people. Somerville would tell the story of a traveler in the cold regions of Tibet, who

> in fear of death on account of the bitter cold, he saw a body of one buried in the snow and at the point of death. He went to this half frozen creature lifting him up on his shoulders, carrying him forward. The efforts he made produced heat in his own body, which passed into the body of the poor victim, and at last he reached shelter where both lives were saved. In saving his fellowman, his own life was saved.[25]

Somerville's evangelical Baptist theology did not lead him toward a concept of salvation through works. One is not saved because of what one does. Instead, he believed those who are saved are obligated to work for the salvation of others. This salvation is holistic—spiritual, physical, relational. Further, missional work results in growth in faith and Christian commitment—the ongoing sanctifying salvation of Christians through the Holy Spirit. One does not work for the salvation of others in order to be saved. One works for the salvation of others because one is saved.

Personal Conversion

The uncompromising evangelical commitment of Somerville was nurtured, in part, by his own conversion. He saw in the testimony of Isaiah, who was encountered by God in the temple, a connection with his own experience. He spoke of a dialogue between God and Isaiah that transformed his life. "Above him he saw the Lord high and lifted up. Around him he saw a people of unclean lips. Underneath him the foundations of the temple shook. All of these were the preamble. The 'real action' took place within him. … One Sunday night I, too, had a dialogue with the Eternal. I had a preacher-father above me, a godly mother around me, but it was not until something took place within me that I am here this hour as a testimony of the Ceaseless Dialogue."[26]

People find their highest possible quality of life in Jesus. By transferring faith from self to Christ, people begin to understand something of God. They begin to discern part of God's purpose and something of humanity's participation in God's purpose for the world.[27] Somerville proclaimed:

> To believe in Christ is to trust the possibilities and to know that what will be is more than what has been. … For it is Christ who goads you to your best, and haunts you at your worst. Yes, He summons you up into what you could be. He forgives you for what you have been. He bids you to laugh at your own insignificance. He causes you to love the unlovable and He causes you to hope when all about is despair. … There is but one way for an individual to find true happiness in this world of ours, and that is to find out the way that Christ is going, and decide to go that way, too.[28]

In a sermon about James, John, and Simon, who left their fishing trade to follow Jesus, Somerville testified:

I thank God that I brought my little ship to land one day when I met the Master, and he said, "follow me and I will make you to become... And I have experienced as I have sought to "become" a hundred, yes, and a thousand times as much sisters, brothers, mother, father, and land-now. And it does not yet appear what I shall eventually become. I only know that, "When I see thee as thou art, I'll praise thee as I ought."[29]

In another sermon about the Samaritan who ministers to the Jewish victim assaulted on the road to Jericho, Somerville bore witness:

I thank God that, at an early age, I became aware that Christ was talking to me when he said, "you too must go and do the same." I was blessed to have a minister father above me. Yes, I was blessed to have a godly mother around me. But it was not until I got Christ in me that I started to accept my divine assignment.[30]

Somerville was unrelenting in his belief in the power of the Gospel for salvation. Salvation is in Christ. The Gospel is transforming. It not only gives eternal life, but it offers answers and remedies to the daily struggles and distress of humanity. He believed Jesus is the answer to all people's ultimate concerns, as well as all the world's problems. Whether high school graduates seeking direction for life, lovers who dream of having a home and children, or parents who aspire for their children's futures, Christ is the answer. This conviction applies to the challenges faced in national and global settings as well-whether racism, hunger, poverty, or war, Christ is the answer. The world continues to echo John's question, "Are you he who is to come, or shall we look for another?" (Luke 7:20) The answer to John's question, as well as to ours, is the impact of Jesus on the lives of the many he touches—the blind now see, the lame now walk, the sick are now healed, the deaf now hear, the dead are raised, and the poor have the good news proclaimed to them. These are missional tasks to which the church and the followers of Christ are called in every age.

Consequently, the question that is implicitly or explicitly asked in every generation finds its affirmative response in the missional engagement of the church in the world.[31]

A Heart for Others

Wendell Somerville was committed to an equitable sharing of all God's resources. He found the exploitation of natural resources and the commitment to the accumulation of much by some contributed to tension around the world. He saw the missional life as a life of faithful stewardship that ensured reasonable distribution to benefit the lives of those living in marginal circumstances. In the 1960s, Somerville proclaimed, that the "basis of all of our problems in ourselves here in Washington, Watts, Harlem, Santo Domingo, Korea, South Africa, Rhodesia, India, China and Vietnam are all the results of the greed, gluttony and insatiable appetites and desires of the 'have gots' to continue to exploit the weak and poor 'have nots' through the world."[32] He was thoroughly convinced that missional living would yield peace in personal, congregational, national, and global contexts. Consequently, he passionately called for "missions instead of missiles" and the valuing of "persons above property."[33]

The call to Christian service in this missional system carries with it the call to sacrifice. The sacrifice required for authentic Christian service, however, also brings with it joy. The motivation for service is the response of God's love for the world through Jesus Christ, and this response prompts the believer to reflect the lifestyle of Christ. So, although joy comes from service, one does not serve in order to receive a "payment" in return. "One's Christianity is determined by the service [one] renders without looking for reward."[34] One service opportunity open to Christians is the giving of one's life in the extraordinary world of missions.

Living into God's missional vision does not allow one to be satisfied with ordinary attainments and accoutrements of success as prescribed by the non-Christian world. Comfortable, luxurious, and fashionable possessions seduce some people to lower their visions of meaningful investment of life. Somerville believed young Americans who had access to education and employment needed to guard themselves against the seductions of accumulation-oriented living that would result in social oppression and economic strangulation. Instead, he challenged young people to discover a task in life that was big enough to demand all of ones' self. Divided loyalties resulted in mediocrity. "The truly great [people] are those who found a big task." And the biggest task and most noble goal for all of life is that of Christian missions.[35]

Somerville consistently urged the church to call forth and send out dedicated and trained young people for global missions. There was a constant great need for them to share with brothers and sisters "across the sea" the gospel message and their practical and technical skills and knowledge. Additionally, he was committed to bringing promising young people to the United States for higher education so they might return to their countries of origin for more effective and comprehensive Christian witness.[36]

Somerville ached for more preachers and pastors committed to a robust global missional agenda, and he passionately pleaded for young men and women to surrender their intellectual, vocational, and spiritual gifts to the global missional call of Christ. People who knew him well frequently witnessed him saying to little boys that God had called them to preach (he was not a proponent of women in ordained preaching ministries). In his own words he confessed: "Everyone who knows me very well is amused over the fact that I try to make a preacher out of every boy I come in contact with. Of course I know that everybody cannot be an ordained preacher. [However,] there is an important place for everyone to fill in the mighty plan of God."[37] This humorous confession points, however, to the consistent commitment of Somerville that it is crucial for the salvation of the world that people personally proclaim the gospel.

Jesus' entire life was one of service and compassion. This is the life his disciples are called to follow.[38] At the core of Wendell Somerville's Christian conviction was that "Christian missions is the one and only essential work of the church."

Missions is not a human creation. Instead, it is the "divine mandate handed down by Jesus Christ." Consequently, every Christian receives a divine assignment to follow Christ in a lifetime commitment to and engagement in missions. When churches allow other activities to substitute for the divine assignment, they cease to express authentic Christianity and simply find themselves "playing religion." [39]

Missions is essential for the church because it continues the work begun in Jesus. In Somerville's thought, Jesus called disciples to live and act in ways he had already begun. Jesus did not complete the purposes of God. He, therefore, sends his disciples into the world to continue his work as the Father had sent him. To be a disciple of Christ is to accept the responsibility to engage constructively the conditions that cause human misery around the world. This includes personal and corporate sin, war, oppression, poverty, and the like.[40]

Using one's life in service to others in need is not born out of a sense of humanism or altruism. It is an outgrowth of the life transformed through Jesus Christ. Somerville understood the life of Jesus as characterized by love and compassion. The love of Christ is a love that invests in the lives of others to the glory of God. The compassion of Christ is demonstrated in generous service that changes one's hopeless circumstances to hopeful new realities. An amazing consequence of living a life consistent with the life of Christ is an unfathomable encounter with joy and ultimate meaning for life.

Every person chosen by Christ is given "the divine assignment" to carry the good news of Jesus to people who need his loving touch. In Somerville's mind, the main task was to go forth and preach the good news in word and deed. The problems of the world he knew were largely due to the priority of preachers to find comfortable places to serve and to stay. He asserted that most preachers were spending the majority of their time on ministry to those who claimed to be saved rather than reaching those who needed the salvation of God in Jesus Christ. This was incomprehensible to the mission minded Somerville.

Somerville unapologetically called Christians to go into the entire world with the Gospel of Jesus Christ. While this call embraced local and global engagement, he never accepted excuses that there was too much to do at home to participate in missions on broader scales. He took his cue from Jesus, who "never waited for the last [person] to be healed, helped or saved in any village before his thoughts went out to those who had never had a chance."[41] The plan of Jesus includes all people, and the church-each congregation-is obligated to participate in the work of Jesus for the redemption of all humanity and to mobilize disciples in this direction.

Gratitude for God's blessings prompts people to respond with missional living. Somerville referred to these people as "The Grateful Minority."[42] Inspired by the story of Jesus healing 10 people with leprosy and a lone Samaritan returning to him with thanksgiving, Somerville lamented the number of African American college graduates who used their liberation from "the terrible scourge of ignorance" to advance their personal wealth and accumulation. Few chose to yield themselves to Christian ministry, social work, and vocational missions that brought light to the dark places of the world. He believed those who were privileged with knowledge were obligated to "let others light their candles by it." This was a responsibility of those benefited with formal education.

Wealth that resulted from professional advancement was not for personal privilege alone. He measured true wealth not by what one possessed but by that which possessed one. He believed excessive material wealth was a curse to most people because it became the priority and measure by which many established value. He illustrated this insight with the following story.

A rich man was standing at the waterfront watching a ship about to sail. "I have on that vessel $10,000.00 worth of equipment for a hospital in China."

"Well," said the other little man, "I also have a gift on that ship. My only daughter is on that vessel going to China to give her life as a missionary."[43]

Somerville's missional stewardship approach was to ask consistently a traditional question in a truer and more penetrating way. Rather than asking "How much of God's money will we give?" the deeper and more profound question is, "How much of God's money will we keep?"[44]

The Adventure of Missions

"The trouble with our generation," Somerville claimed, "is that people are trying to live a maximum life on a minimum faith."[45] He recognized a contradiction in the way Christians lived compared to the biblical account of Caleb, who was ready to possess the mountain Horeb that Moses had promised him for his faithfulness (ref. Numbers 13-14). While possessing mountains is difficult, it is also exhilarating. Mountain climbing is not easy, but both the experience of the climb as well as the success of the feat offer tremendous reward. Regrettably, too many Christians failed to attempt to scale the mountains of the missional adventure in favor of the safety and predictability of the valleys of religious routine.

> Most Christians today have valley religion. They worship in a comfortable church, hear great sermons, listen to fine robed choirs. All of this is good, but it is valley religion.
>
> As you sit today in your valley religion, two out of three persons in the world went to bed last night without enough to eat. Three out of four persons in the world are without Christ. People are exploited and emaciated in Africa. Millions of Indians are submerged in a bloody strife. Bleeding China and impoverished Haiti all call to us in the valley to come up out of the valley to the mountain and experience *mountain religion* (emphasis in the original).[46]

Missions draws the Christian into it. Being missional is an outgrowth of discipleship. Being missional is irresistible for the maturing follower of Christ. Recalling a visit to a leprosy colony, Somerville spoke of asking Dr. George Harley whether he was afraid of contracting leprosy from patients he treated. Harley replied, "I am much more afraid of not doing my duty as the Lord has shown it to me."[47] Somerville echoed this sentiment through his testimony that "People are my business. My Master put me into it a long time ago, and I cannot quit it without betraying my master."[48]

Christian missions goes beyond duty, however. It invigorated Somerville. To follow Christ and to participate in his redeeming work of humanity is to embark on an exciting journey of faith. The biblical record attests to the fact that those who follow Jesus daily can anticipate the new and unpredictable.[49] Being missional is a result of obedience, service, and consecration, however, missions is more than mere obligation. He saw following Christ in missional living as a great adventure. He admired missionaries whom he knew, befriended, and supported as embarking on great adventures with Christ.[50]

Referring to a spiritually and emotionally intense visit to India, Somerville wrote:

> After several hours of visitation in the squalored slums of filth, suffering and misery among the physical and social lepers, I asked what we could do. Rev. and Dr. Nelson replied: "If you supply us with medicines, we will inject these cankered and diseased bodies with antibiotics. If you will help us to provide food to fill these swollen and abnormal bellies of these little children, we will seek to remove their hunger. If you will provide us with textbooks and blackboards, we will enlighten their minds. If you will support us with your funds and prayers, we will declare the glorious Good News of a Risen Christ, who came that all men may have life and have it more abundantly."[51]

Referring to an encounter with Ivy Nelson, one of Lott Carey's physicians in New Delhi, India, while kneeling at the bedside of decaying bodies of victims of leprosy, Somerville asked if she was not afraid of contracting leprosy. He recorded her response as: "Jesus says 'Follow me,' and he sets us to tasks that he has to fulfill for our time. No individual can know ahead exactly what [role that one] will be asked to play in the tasks that God has to fulfill in our time. But a decision must be made since Jesus leaves no place to hide, for he is a universal figure with worldwide dimensions."[52]

Missions is not only a personal adventure. It also is a cooperative venture where Christians join God in redeeming the world. This redemption is holistic. It speaks to the whole of the human predicament. It must address the interior and the exterior needs of humanity. God is redeeming the soul of humanity, and God is redeeming the human predicaments of poverty, hunger, homelessness, injustice, illiteracy, and threat of military annihilation. The work of the redemption of the entire world to God, however, is not God's work alone. It also belongs to followers of Christ. It is the business of Christians. Somerville held that the business of missions was particularly the task of Christians who lived in the United States because of their privileges and affluence. These resources should be used to respond to the needs of the impoverished around the world. This kind of missional living means that meeting the internal and external conditions of people is God's business, and it is ours, too.[53]

Somerville advanced the "healing" nature of Christian missions. "Wherever is found churches, schools, homes, hospitals, orphanages, respect for womanhood, care for children, protection of the weak, reverence for the old, and respect and dignity of human personality, Christian missions has played an important role."[54] This healing nature of Christian missions related to Somerville's conviction that tangible "signs" validate faithful service. This is not to say that outputs prove the faithfulness of missional work. Examples abound of missionaries who have toiled faithfully without realizing their desired outcomes. Yet, Somerville continued to assert his conviction that God gives increase in relationship to those who plant and water in God's time and way.[55]

Missional living calls for creative thinking. The global reach of Christ's missional command demands thinking beyond conventional ideas. Conventional thinking limits possibilities. His era demanded imagination and innovation. Somerville preached as early as the 1960s: "Juvenile thinking cannot compete with our radar age. After all, this world is ruled by ideas." Additionally, he declared: "Our present supersonic age of jets and automation requires men and women who can *think big thoughts* (emphasis in the original)." Jesus issued his disciples a "spiritual passport that contained a mission and a destiny that transcended all racial and geographical boundaries." Somerville urged Christians to enlarge their vision of their world geographically. But he also encouraged expanded vision in sympathy with the poor, the illiterate, the sick, and those without Christ globally.[56]

Evangelism

Wendell Clay Somerville frequently referred to Matthew 11:2-6 in sermons. He saw in John's question sent to Jesus—whether he was the Christ or should they look for another—a lamp flickering in John's life that reflects the flickering of faith that all people experience in life. The answer is given by evidence of Jesus' work. Healing the sick, restoring the dead, and preaching good news to the poor were evidence that Jesus was the Christ. Somerville saw healing, empowering, and preaching as definitive signs of the living Christ in the lives of churches and Christians.

Christianity, for Somerville, only had value as it was shared with others. Many people that claimed to be Christians tried to contain Jesus within their traditions and cultures. Christianity has power only when it is shared. Otherwise, it is simply rhetorical. Appreciative and respectful of all people who lived with character and commitment to care for and improve the lives of those that were vulnerable to exploitation and that were victimized by those with disproportionate amounts of wealth and might (for example, he greatly admired the life and work of Gandhi), Somerville was unapologetically evangelical in his confidence in Jesus as the answer to humanity's deepest needs. In his own words, "I, too, once thought that moral goodness, character education, and sociology would solve all our problems....I have since discovered that there is more power and strength in the simple name of Jesus than all of the textbooks and social theories ever written."[57]

Somerville's missional thrust was thoroughly evangelistic. "I challenge you today," he proclaimed, "to remember that the God of Jesus Christ has called us to save the world."[58] He took seriously the call to declare to the world that Jesus saves, and that salvation is holistic. Although he valued the work of all people that made this world more humane and habitable for the most vulnerable, good work for a common good was not the aim of Christian people. He believed the orientation of Christian living is toward "the other," and that this is consistent with the biblical witness of the life and work of Jesus.

He contended that a unique characteristic of Jesus was that he consistently reached out to others. He reached out to sinners, the sick, and the marginalized by culture. "The strength of our religion is manifested in the amount we share with others." Somerville claimed. He saw this principle in the story of Jesus' encounter with the Samaritan woman at Jacob's well (John 4). Although she had only recently met Jesus in a midday encounter at a well, she acted on her newfound faith and moved a city to meet Jesus. This stood in contrast to the disciples of Jesus who, upon discovering Jesus in conversation with this "other" woman of Samaria, struggled to grasp what Jesus was doing. Their constant companionship with Jesus did not translate into a reaching out to others. In contrast, the instant relationship with the Samaritan woman at the well produced an enthusiastic and persuasive missional response. Again, in Somerville's words, "It is not important as to the amount of religion you posses. The important thing is how much you use."

Somerville held that God intended salvation for the world. As a Christian and U.S. citizen, he believed the North American church possessed a unique opportunity to serve

God's purpose for redemption. He retained this confident testimony despite the racial inequities and brutalities inflicted on those of his ethnicity that often happened with either sanction or silence from the majority of the Anglo American church. "Our own United States," Somerville declared, "could qualify as God's instrument of world redemption if she were willing to set her house in order." [59]

In more than one sermon, however, he contended that God was able to bring deliverance from another quarter should the Christian church refuse to engage the world. While affirming the biblical witness that Christians are workers together with God, he simultaneous claimed that, "If we fail him, God shall not fail. Remember, whenever people fulfill his ethical demands, they are his chosen people. He can take that remnant and build his world."[60]

Was Somerville serious? Did he actually believe God could use a path other than the Christian church to reach the world for salvation? Was this claim homiletic hyperbole or serious conviction? While this position is not a major thrust of his preaching and teaching, it is probably an error to dismiss the intent of his statement out of hand. Somerville probably meant exactly what he said. He was unrelenting in his life commitment to exalting the name of Jesus around the world and reaching people holistically with the Gospel of Christ in every conceivable way. He also was unyielding in his assertion that God's will could not be derailed by the failure of Christian people to live up to Christ's evangelical commands. Ultimately, Somerville was committed to the sovereignty of God to speak, act, and redeem the world through whatever avenues God may choose. This conclusion, however, in no way reduced his unremitting devotion to an evangelical missional witness around the world and his absolute conviction that this privilege and duty was assigned to disciples of Jesus Christ.

God's grace is not limited to any particular race or group. Jesus says if anyone will come after me, one must deny self, take up his or her cross and follow Jesus. Somerville took this universal invitation seriously. This gave theological underpinning to his passion for global missions.[61] His preaching indicated a keen awareness for people globally. He frequently referred to the pain and marginalization of people east and west, north and south. All Christians should be committed to authentic holistic expressions of the Gospel everywhere. This was an essential test of discipleship. Is the one who professes to follow Christ engaged in missional witness to the whole of the human condition-spiritual, physical, relational, psychological, economical, political? Referring to Jesus' message of Matthew 25 and the final judgment, Somerville argued that we are tested regularly. And Christians must pass the test of ministering to the temporal as well as eternal needs of people. This message is particularly critical for those who live in affluence in the United States.

"To those who say that they follow Jesus, I would remind you that you cannot have Jesus and reject his program of missions. … Jesus says follow me! And he sets before us the tasks that he must accomplish in our time. He commands and to those who listen to him, wise and unwise, he will reveal himself in the peace, the labor, the conflicts, the suffering which they must experience in his company, and as an inexpressible mystery they will learn who he is."[62] Elsewhere, Somerville proclaimed that every Christian is a missionary, and that "Salvation must turn us from a life centered on ourselves toward a life going out toward God and [humankind]. In other words, one cannot believe in Christ without accepting His program for humanity."[63]

The Missional Strategy

Wendell Clay Somerville believed the work of missions had to be done with a keen awareness of and engagement with the broader social realities of each age. This approach enabled missional relevance. Relevant missional strategies functioned amid rapid technological and societal transformation. They also had to address the fact that many world views challenged the assumption that Christianity was considered credible and commendable. Missional relevance called for the appropriate stewardship of resources. Missional strategic significance demanded attention to issues of gender equality. These issues and more called for meaningful and insightful missional thinking and living.

Missional Relevance

In 1958, Somerville addressed the ominous launch of Sputnik III. This event poignantly highlighted the incredible potential for good that could come from human advances, but it also raised the threatening potential for devastation. "At last," he wrote, "we have come to the stage where [people have] succeeded in guiding powerful missiles. The inherent danger of all of this is the fact that we have guided missiles, but they are in the hands of misguided men. ... In the midst of this confusion of guided missiles and misguided men, the non-Christian world has a perfect right to turn to us of the Christian faith and ask in the words of Zedekiah, 'Is there a word from the Lord?'"[1] Somerville's answer was an unqualified "yes."

Christian missions needed to be done particularly where the integrity of the Christian community was questioned. International perception about American Christianity called for a substantive missional witness relevant to the complexities of people's lives. Somerville was once asked through hilarious laughter by African students traveling to Russia, China, and East Germany to continue academic studies, "How can you have Christ in your heart, with a nuclear bomb in your hand?"[2]

Somerville believed churches must share their affluence with those who are afflicted. This was not optional. It was essential for a credible Christian witness through the church. In a note of chastisement in 1973, Somerville wrote, "Many of our churches are floating on the clouds of affluence with their modern air-conditioned auditoriums, wall-to-wall carpet on the floors, and their various auxiliaries working overtime, *doing church work* (emphasis in the original). The masses of the 'other brothers' through the world are scurrying about with unbearable burdens of affliction."[3]

Somerville was an unrelenting advocate for significant investments in Christian mission. He warned against the distractions of secularism and materialism to the church. He longed to see the contemporary church regain the passion the early church had for evangelism. He had an amazingly contemporary sounding critique of churches as early as the mid-1940s. "Many of our churches are so anxious to become 'uplift' agencies and social centers that many have degenerated into glorified USA Clubs. Any church that uses more money for its so-called operating expenses than it contributes to Christian missions is neglecting the weightier matter and is majoring in minors. Whenever secularism enters the local church, that church loses its voice and power in speaking the words of Christ to a lost generation."[4]

Somerville consistently lavished praise upon women who were leaders and supporters of missions through Lott Carey. Early in his tenure he expressed appreciation for the tremendous character and generosity of women involved in missions with the organization. Simultaneously, however, he expressed disappointment that the organization had not tapped into the vast reservoir of potential that resided in women of Lott Carey churches. He believed the Lott Carey organization of the early 1940s needed to think more creatively about how to mobilize the "thousands of well-trained, cultured, and consecrated women in our churches" who were not actively engaged in missions. "I have deep and abiding faith in the ability, vision and consecration of the women of the Women's Auxiliary." Somerville believed the creativity employed by secular organizations to recruit and deploy young women into their service (e.g. military agencies like the Women's Army Corps during World War II) should inspire the church to exercise greater imagination to engage gifted young women for its cause. He held the same conviction regarding the need to use ingenuity to enlist young people into the mission enterprise.[5]

A relevant missional strategy for Somerville included personal, congregational, and societal dimensions. We have already explored his concept of the missional church and the missional life. The missional focus of his work and thought also leads to missional engagements in societal contexts. In order to execute a biblically driven missional enterprise personally, congregationally, and collaboratively, one must apply it socially. This pertains to how one implements an evangelical program, as well as one's approach to the political realities of the world—particularly in relationship to those who suffer from disenfranchisement, inequality, and marginalization. Consequently, to follow a missional direction proposed by Wendell Somerville, one must include holistic and political dimensions. Holism, in this system, refers to a robust approach to the human community that values the entirety of people's existences. To focus on the interior life exclusively is not authentic evangelism in this approach. Missional engagement requires attention to the whole of human existence at the personal and political levels. To speak of politics in this approach, however, is not to speak of a debased partisanship that often characterizes interactions between parties, ethnicities, and nations. Politics here relates to the realities of interactions between people and groups of people.

Holistic Evangelism

The key elements of missions advanced by Wendell Clay Somerville included evangelism, education, health, and industry.[6] While these priorities took shape with greater definition as he matured in his role as a mission executive, he advanced a holistic understanding of missions beginning with his first Annual Report issued in 1941. Referring to the work of Lott Carey missions in Liberia and Haiti under the direction of W. H. Thomas and Boaz A. Harris respectively, Somerville wrote: "These servants are on the Christian battlefront fighting ignorance, idolatry, sin and disease ...."[7] At the start of his ministry in "foreign missions," Somerville articulated a multifaceted understanding of missions. I cannot document when he came to this awareness, but he both embraces and advances the large horizon of missions he met upon arriving at Lott Carey in 1940.

Somerville believed people involved in missions should possess a zeal for evangelism along with the passion and capacity for helping improve life in other ways where they served. In 1941, Somerville articulated a future goal of Lott Carey to select missionaries "on the basis of their Christian devotion and *specialized training in some distinct field* [emphasis in the original].[8] In a 1948 report to Lott Carey leadership following a two-month visit to Lott Carey missionaries in Liberia, Haiti, and Bermuda, Somerville criticized the failure of adequate selection and supervision of missionaries by various foreign mission boards in the United States. Missionaries, he believed, should have a high level of spiritual passion as well as secular preparation.

By 1977, Somerville had crystallized his principles for missions. He contended:

> Our first priority is that of *evangelism*. We think of evangelism as the promulgation of the good news of the redemption of mankind through Jesus Christ. ...

Our second priority is that of education—*enlightening the minds*. ... At each of the mission stations we emphasize the importance of enlightening the mind; and, we seek to instill in the minds of our youth two kinds of education. One [educational emphasis] is to teach one how to make a living, and the other how to live. ... Our third objective has been that of *ministering to the health* needs of our indigent brothers and sisters throughout the dark places of the earth.[9]

Evangelism

Wendell Somerville was committed to winning people to Jesus Christ through authentic witness, preaching, and living. His commitment to the Bible as authoritative for faith and life grounded his missional vision. His compassion for people, especially for people who were poor and oppressed, stirred his energy and zeal. He constantly expressed devotion to sharing the gospel to the world. The social, economic, militaristic, and political challenges seen during his service as a missional leader were sobering, but they did not deter his determination. The competition of other faith systems for the hearts and minds of people were clear, but he did not shrink from an unapologetic passion for the Christian witness.

Somerville was an evangelical. Framing the results of a fact-finding report that Lott Carey commissioned in 1984 to study the contemporary contexts of the organization's international partnerships and to recommend actions to enhance and enlarge its missionary program, Somerville declared "our *bottom line is* to lead people to know how to know Christ Jesus" (emphasis in the original)[10]. The mature Somerville shows remarkable consistency through the years in his clarity of priority for evangelism. He wrote in 1944:

The compelling force, which has undergirded the program of the Lott Carey Convention from its incipiency, has been that of sharing our personally experienced fellowship with Jesus Christ with other men in other lands. Our message has been that of complete and total reclamation of the whole [person]. We have sought to carry this message of salvation through the method of preaching, teaching, healing. … At each of our stations the importance of preaching is constantly emphasized. The question, "How can they hear without a preacher?" is still important and vital.[11]

Evangelism was fundamental in missions to Somerville. Proclaiming the good news that Jesus is the Savior of the world was central. His evangelical understanding of missions, however, was more robust than preaching and establishing churches.

> Surely, the prime motive of any missionary enterprise must be that of a deep and abiding inner desire to religiously share one's talents and energies for his less fortunate brothers [and sisters], however, the time has come that missionary-candidates must possess other vital characteristics, in addition to spiritual fervor.[12]

Missions was grounded in evangelism but not bounded by it. Somerville's strategy for missions was a multifaceted enterprise. Somerville had an amazingly broad definition of Christian missions in the middle of the 20th Century when he would write:

> The present year of 1957 completes a period of sixty years that the Lott Carey Baptist Foreign Mission Convention has constantly sought to play its part in setting forth the fact that world tensions, brutality and unbrotherly attitudes between men and groups are all the fruits of human sin.
>
> Therefore, we have relentlessly endeavored to send forth Christian missionaries into the various parts of the world with the healing message of salvation. For the most part, these consecrated missionaries are reaching people of all races with the transforming power of the Gospel of Jesus Christ. They are establishing schools and teaching

in them; they are providing clinics and ministering to the sick; they are seeking to improve methods of farming; they are studying foreign languages and cultures, opening communications, forming friendships, mediating the shock of change, serving tribes in the interior, assisting townspeople and migrants in the city, and promoting social justice in such matters as wages, welfare and housing. In all of this they express our "Christian concern with life in its wholeness."[13]

By 1971, Somerville was continuing his claim that evangelism was essential to the life of the church and its mission around the world. Despite the bewildering experiences of scientific discoveries, new morality standards, the sexual revolution, substance abuse, and "use of our monster killing machines," Somerville heralded the place of the gospel for the world in expressly Trinitarian language. "Unfortunately," he lamented, "our generation fails to understand the way of life as taught by Jesus Christ is relevant for all time. His principle of love, honesty, unselfishness and purity are dateless. They are applicable for yesterday, today and all tomorrows; and, furthermore, our Christian behavior depends on our communion with the eternal God, our experience with the risen Christ and our being led by the Holy Spirit."[14]

Education

Education in the missionary enterprise was a priority for Somerville. Education was not for intellectual enlightenment alone or knowledge for the sake of knowledge. There was a functional purpose for education. Education was essential for liberation from oppression. Exploited people around the world needed education as a tool to greater security and self-reliance. "The Lott Carey Baptist Foreign Mission Convention has constantly held that Christianity and education are inseparable. Along with our program of evangelism has gone the process of education. … We hold that literacy opens doors of bondage. 'He who reads leads.'

When the minds of [people] are liberated, no power on earth can keep them enslaved. Exploitation can exist only where [people] are poor and ignorant."[15]

Early in his tenure, Somerville demonstrated an understanding of the excessive burden that women bore in already oppressed communities. Committing to educational opportunities for girls was a result of his insight and was intended to begin a systemic approach to liberation for women. On a 1943 visit to Haiti, Somerville wrote,

> I was terribly stirred by the impoverished condition of the peasant masses. The peasant women in particular seemed to offer the greatest challenge to our Christian conscience. To that end the school which we erected in St. Marc was designed to give the peasant girls and women the "first chance" to get an education which would lift them up from their places of dejection and defenselessness.[16]

Education also was connected to "industry." Somerville viewed industry, the creation of jobs and economic viability, as part of the missionary enterprise. Work was integrally related to one's well being. All missionaries during the 1950s era of Lott Carey's work were expected to pledge to a principle of work and industry. Somerville was cautious, however, to distinguish his position on the importance of industry from that of others of the day. He contended:

> we do not feel that the mere ability to develop an industry will relieve us as Christians in the continuance of sharing our best with peoples of these economically liberated areas. The lessons of [World War II] have taught us that mere economic independence does not make and keep a people happy and safe.
>
> There are those today who would have us believe that our chief duty is to make backward people economically free, and then our task is complete. The mere possession of material wealth gives no assurance of freedom. ... Wealth without

knowledge—how to direct this wealth for the services of mankind is not only useless but is dangerous.[17]

Health

Health was emphasized in two ways. First, the organization only launched ambitious programs of hospitalization when it was able to adequately support them. Sustainability seemed to be a crucial area of concern for Somerville. Second, missionaries were required to be equipped for basic medical and nursing service.[18]

Somerville led the Lott Carey organization to begin a sustained investment in India in the 1940s that included education, evangelism, and health. The missional leaders were a pastor and his physician spouse whose commitment and competence to Somerville's holistic understanding of the Gospel impressed and inspired him deeply through the years. One of his recollections of working with Rev. Abner and Dr. Ivy Nelson communicates something of Somerville's passion for healing as an integral part of any global evangelistic thrust.

I recently saw an impossible dream fulfilled in India as I watched Dr. Ivey Nelson toiling night and day among the poor, neglected, and suffering lepers. I asked why she was identifying herself among this horde of miserable creatures when she could be serving in one of the modern hospitals. She replied, "I was head of one of the leading hospitals in Delhi, but as I observed the lost host of lepers that could not receive any type of medical service because of their horrible disease, I fell on my knees and asked God for the impossible. If he would provide an opening for me, I would give up my present position and would devote my life to work among the lepers. Then the Lott Carey Convention came and offered me this glorious privilege."

As I watched her kneeling at the side of one leper after another, I inquired if she were not afraid of contracting this dreadful disease. She arose and with a smile on her face and a gleam in her eye said: "Jesus says, 'Follow me!' and he sets us to tasks that he has to fulfill for our time. No individual can know ahead exactly what part God has to fulfill for our time, but one who accepts the assignment will discover who Jesus really is."[19]

Somerville challenged the Lott Carey community to engage in the battle against AIDS as early as 1987. This is impressive given the lack of attention the pandemic was then receiving among Christian communities in the U.S. and the fact that he was 87 years old at the time. He wrote: "It is imperative that the Lott Carey Baptist Foreign Mission Convention will immediately proceed to secure funds to forward to [the Southern African countries of Zaire, Zambia, Burundi, Rwanda, Mozambique and Tanzania] to assist in the research agencies to find a cure for this deadly disease. For the church can never be neutral on human or moral issues, for the Divine maxim of Jesus Christ is, *it is always right to do right* (emphasis in the original).[20]

Politics, Race, and the World

Somerville had an amazingly global vision as early as 1940. He was reluctant to offer public analyses of international affairs early in his global missional leadership role. That reluctance, however, would yield to insightful assessments and prophetic critique in later years. His first report to the Lott Carey Convention made clear reference to international disturbances of the early 1940s. He used great nuance to address global realities yet succeeded in communicating his sentiments about the need for judicial consideration regarding issues of war.

Both isolationists and interventionists are found actively defending their positions. Ever since its organization in 1897, the Lott Carey Baptist Foreign Mission Convention has followed a policy of non-activity in economic, civic and political issues, therefore I shall not attempt to give either an official or an individual expression at this time. However, it is obvious to all who proclaim the name of Christian that fear and faith cannot remain in the same heart at the same time; and, as followers of the Christ of God, Christians everywhere would do well to take counsel of and ponder the words of Jesus as stated thus, "I come that they may have life, and that they might have it more abundantly." He further says, "For all they that take the sword shall perish with the sword."[21]

A decade following Somerville's appointment to serve as Executive Secretary of the Lott Carey Convention, he offered more clearly defined observations about international politics. By 1950, some were asserting World War III had started with what came to be known in the United States as the Korean Conflict. Somerville called for deep contemplation among Christians globally concerning their complicity with the global tragedies of the era. "Christians and the so-called civilized leaders must assume full responsibility for the present chaos. Millions of human beings throughout the world have lost faith in our so-called civilization. These people are learning new ways of meeting their suffering and oppressions."[22]

Somerville, consistent with many Christians of his era, saw the ideals of Western civilization and the ideals of Christianity as linked closely together. His sentiment was related to a well-intentioned concept many of his contemporaries held: Christianity would greatly enhance civilization. "It is our responsibility," he claimed in 1950, "to decide if an era is to dawn in the transformation of the present social order into the Kingdom of God, or if western civilization is to take its place in the graveyard of dead civilization and God will have to try all over once more."[23] Of course, these were Western ideas of civilization. While similar in language, his embrace of this concept differed substantially from many of his white American contemporaries. There are many elements of his thought that point in other directions.

His emphasis on the need for Christianity to support the independence movements of African countries contradicts the dominant American and European Christian commitments of his day. Incredibly few Christian leaders voiced support for budding independent African states. Little support was given to efforts to throw off colonial imperialism and to support indigenous self-determination and self-reliance. His further insistence on the crucial, even essential, role of the American Negro in global Christianity and successful Western political diplomacy flew in the face of the prevailing opinions of his era. American Negroes were subject to discrimination, oppression, marginalization, and institutionalized violence through most of Somerville's life. Non-black Christian voices rarely called for the full liberation and affirmation of American Negroes during Somerville's life. Additionally, Somerville's unrelenting commitment to democracy, irrespective of whether outcomes agreed or disagreed with U.S. foreign policy, differentiated him from his Anglo contemporaries. He understood that oppressed people, given the opportunity to decide their direction, might well choose leaders who represent radically different commitments than their oppressors. These new directions also could be threatening to the will of U.S. strategic, political, and economic interests. However, if the people choose that to be, Somerville's thought held, so be it.

Somerville held failures of Western Christianity significantly responsible for the rise of Communism. In 1950, he wrote: "The effectiveness of Communism lies chiefly in the fact that it seems to offer the exploited and neglected peoples of the world what has been denied them in a civilization that has often regarded itself as Christian. Many of these frustrated peoples turn to Communism because they feel that it is a quicker way to achieving the better life."[24] He further challenged traditional and hegemonic notions of "civilization" by pointing to the use of the atomic bomb on Nagasaki and Hiroshima as well as Congress' willingness to approve billions of dollars on militarism to show the goodness of democracy, while simultaneously failing to pass legislation that would "remove the economic strangulation from the necks of America's largest minority."[25]

The mature Somerville continued to understand the role of missions as engaging people with a clear and keen awareness of global systemic contexts. By 1986, the octogenarian set forth a concise, yet prophetic, call for international moral responsibility. Given his conviction that Christians should have global visions of missions that the Gospel would be preached through the entire world, he wrote:

> [I]t is obvious that Christian Mission is related to and involved in all human and moral issues such as: a) The abolition of all nuclear weapons, b) the ratification of the SALT II Treaty, c) To seek to equalize the natural resources among all people, d) To ratify the U.N. Peace Resolution, and e) To denounce and repudiate the horrible Apartheid system of segregation.[26]

Pan-African Politics

Somerville was a man in tune with the struggles of African people around the world. His awareness led him to a deep commitment for the liberation struggle of people on the African continent. He was convinced that Christianity was essential to the liberation of African people. The Christianity that would bring liberty, however, was not a narrow kind of Christianity that sought only the salvation of the soul. His brand of Christianity was holistic. The holism that characterized Somerville's concept of Christianity would give Africans the tools they needed to combat what he saw as tri-dimensional threats that included nationalism, Islam, and Communism. To this end, he consistently lifted Lott Carey's historic banner, "Building a Better World through Christian Missions."

Somerville was an early proponent of connecting American Negroes with their African siblings. He made an incredibly forward thinking observation in 1946:

The future welfare of the American Negro is inextricably associated with the Black Republic of Liberia. Liberia stands today at her crossroads. There are unlimited possibilities both for the Negroes of America and the people of Liberia, if both will manifest sufficient judgment and understanding so as to mutually share each other's resources of mind, soul and intelligence in making Liberia a modern state. It is my sincere hope that the Negroes of America will immediately realize how badly Liberia needs them as doctors, dentists, teachers, merchants, agriculturists, skilled artisans and friends; and, Liberia offers them her untapped and unfathomed resources of both material wealth and brilliant intellects.[27]

Beyond the pragmatism of linking American Negroes with African people was a deeper connection. Somerville saw an existential link that could not be denied, no matter how hard some may have tried. He contended: "Regardless how strenuously many American Negroes try to disassociate themselves from the people of Africa, the fact still remains that every American Negro has his genealogy in those former slaves who were brought into this new world against their wills." This existentialism was not born of pure emotion. Somerville was a proponent of the centrality of Africa to human civilization and the science that supported this claim. He advanced this notion as early as 1951: "It is generally conceded by men of science that Africa is the ancient seat of civilization; and modern society as we know it today, had its origin in the heart of this vast domain."[28] To advance this unique connection between American Negroes and African people, the Lott Carey Convention organized a 1951 "African Pilgrimage." A key goal of the pilgrimage was to facilitate interaction and understanding among numbers of American Negroes, most of whom would have been affiliated with the Lott Carey Convention, and a number of African people, most of whom were Liberian.[29]

Somerville introduced his 1958-1959 annual report with reflections on the plight and possibilities of African people and their leaders. Somerville quotes the British historian Arnold J. Toynbee as saying: "The one hope of Western Civilization is a rebirth of the Christian Spirit; and, it will be the Negro that will rekindle that spirit." Toynbee's opinion resonated with Somerville's conviction. Somerville proceeded to mention a few dynamic African leaders worthy of commendation and serious consideration. Among them were Kenya's Jomo Kenyatta; Guinea's Sekou Toure; Ghana's Kwame Nkrumah; Liberia's W.V.S Tubman; Nigeria's Dr. Nnamdi Azikiue; Nyasaland's Dr. Hastings Banda; and Kenya's youthful 28-year-old Tom Mboya.[30] Emphasizing his liberationist political posture and the critical role and responsibility African Americans held in the struggle, he continued,

> One who has just returned from a ten thousand mile visit through Africa has said, "In all lands the black man is on the move, rushing he is not sure where, but shouting the great word UHURU, (Freedom)!" The officials of the Lott Carey Baptist Foreign Mission Convention are cognizant of this cry, UHURU, for we too have for 340 years "sat where they sat;" and, it has been through the power and grace of Him who said, "When the Son sets you free, you are sure enough free," that we have dedicated our time, talents, prayers, and money in seeking to break the economic, social, moral, and spiritual shackles of our fellowman throughout the whole world.[31]

Somerville took great pride in the rapid progress toward independence African countries made. There were just a few independent countries on the continent when he first visited Africa in 1944. By the time he made an around-the-world visit to 19 countries in 1960, there were 30 independent nations in Africa.[32]

He seemed to have a particular fondness for Liberia. This affection was from two sources. First, Liberia was a pioneer in African statehood, having the longest continuous history as an independent African country. Second, Rev. Lott Carey led a pioneer team of Baptist missionaries in 1821—the first Baptist missionaries to go to Africa from the United States—that settled in Liberia where Carey would be the organizing pastor of Liberia's first Baptist church (Providence Baptist Church) as well as serve as a governmental leader. The following sentiment fairly represents Somerville's fondness for Liberia.

> For more than a hundred years, Liberia had to struggle against the powerful forces of British and French politics and strategy. These countries constantly gnawed at the borders of Liberia attempting to swallow her up in their greedy empires. Thanks to the vision and foresight of the early Liberian leaders who put their trust in the Eternal God and at the same time sought to acquaint themselves with legal understanding and jurisprudence as they presented their case before the world court. As a matter of fact, it has been the legal genius developed as a result of struggle that stands out in Liberia's signal history.[33]

No doubt, Somerville's affection for Liberia was additionally influenced by the obvious appreciation felt by the Liberian government for the educational contributions made by the Lott Carey Convention. Until the 1950s, the Lott Carey Mission School was the only accredited high school operated by African Americans in the country of Liberia. The Liberian government recognized the substantial contributions the Lott Carey Convention made to the country by giving it 1,500 acres of fertile land to develop and on which to expand its missional and educational programs.[34]

While Liberia clearly held a special place in the heart of Wendell Somerville, he deeply admired other African people and leaders who were valiantly struggling to establish their places as equal citizens of the world. Referring to a 1960 visit to Ghana, he wrote:

> The leaders of Ghana are intelligent, alert and are conscious of the roles which they are expected to play in the New Africa. As we began making preparation

to leave Ghana for our next African stop, a brief spell of inquietude came over me in the thought that I could not remain longer in this significant area where revolutionary changes are taking place. These are social changes that within the next ten years will completely modify the current conception of Africa as the "dark Continent." It is indeed an exhilarating experience to stand on the site where history is being made."[35]

Nigeria impressed Somerville as a potential leader among African nations for two reasons. First, the enormous population of Nigeria (some 40 million people in 1960) meant it was positioned for leadership. Somerville saw Nigeria as a linchpin in the formation of a West African economic block that could supply materials to the rest of the world. This economic arrangement would boost the standard of living and political capital of the region, as well as the continent. Second, Somerville saw Nigeria as a potential military power in the region. Given the rise in atomic and nuclear weaponry, he saw Nigeria as bringing the kind of presence that would establish international clout. Military parity also would bring economic, political, and social advance for the region.[36]

Somerville's 1960 visit to Africa was instructive for him in important ways. The opportunity to visit several countries and interact with African people and leaders across national borders led him to a clearer conception of African realities. While, as an American of African heritage, he could not fully understand the depth and breadth of everything he witnessed, he enlarged his understanding of then growing concepts on the continent, such as African presence, African personality, and Negritude. Additionally, he was introduced to the ideas of Africanisation and Pan-Africanism.

Somerville's growing knowledge and appreciation for Pan-Africanism is evident in his 1963 reflections on that year's conference in Addis Ababa, Ethiopia to form the Organization of African Unity. He refers to the conference as a modern miracle in that, despite the fact that these thirty-one leaders represented more than six hundred (600) languages and dialects, they experienced a modern Pentecost in that they united into one great voice in formulating a compact, which represented a United States of Africa. These determined men came together with an unparalleled purpose to put in motion an economic, political and social machine that will transform all Africa into a modern statecraft. ... It was President Nkrumah who seemed to summarize the theme and hope of these Pan-African leaders. He said that "Africans must integrate their economic plans, seek to unify their military strategy and to coordinate their foreign policy and diplomacy."[37]

He goes on to rejoice in the "refreshing breath of freedom" emerging from Africa that had been coined in the word Harambee—meaning pulling together or working together.[38]

Somerville believed the 1960s was a time ripe with possibilities for the American Negro on the international stage. Citing wisdom attributed to the Chinese general Sun Tzu two millennia earlier who, incidentally, would have been a contemporary of the philosopher Confucius, Somerville believed: "The people are the water and the ruler is the boat. The water can support the boat, but it can also sink it." Somerville sensed the millions of marginalized and disenfranchised people around the world represent the "have nots," and that they may be about to turn against the "have gots." Therefore, "it may be providential that the American Negro Christian has 'come to the Kingdom for such a time as this.'"[39]

Race and Missions

The call for the Christian community was to carry the good news of Jesus Christ into the entire world. Sharing this message involved both words and deeds. Deeds would impact individual lives, communities, and the larger society.

Somerville did not harbor illusions of Lott Carey placing missionary personnel in every part of the world that needed to hear the Gospel. He did, however, believe every effort must be made to fulfill Lott Carey's integral part among foreign missionaries from the United States and Canada who served Christ around the world.

Wendell Clay Somerville believed in the strength and the possibilities of black people both in the United States and in Africa. He articulated early an audacious goal for "the only Convention of its kind in the world among Negro Baptists" because of its specialization in "foreign missions" and with whom there was "no rivalry or competition between the Lott Carey Convention and any other local or national organization."[40] His eighth goal presented in his first annual report to the Lott Carey Convention in 1941 read:

> As soon as reasonably possible the Lott Carey Baptist Foreign Mission Convention will extend its sphere of activities into wider areas such as China, India, South America, Russia, and other non-Christian foreign communities. The Lott Carey Convention has a prophetic Christian message not only for "darker races" but for the entire world. We believe that the world is the field and our message is a world message.[41]

He was inspired by the impressive position of self-sustainability and autonomy the Lott Carey Convention held among mission organizations. He noted in 1945 that "the entire income of this Convention is derived from Negroes. Our total constituency is made up of Afro-Americans." He noted in 1950 that, "One of the most natural emotions of the Negro is that of sympathy towards the oppressed. It is no accident that the American Negroes, though often living on the border-line of economic insecurity, have generously given their time, talent and money to the cause of foreign missions. More than ¾ of a million dollars was contributed last year by American Negroes for foreign missions through various churches and Boards."[42] In 1950, the average household income of African Americans was

$1,869, as compared to the average household income of white Americans of $3,335.[43]

While he was proud of Lott Carey's capacity as an African American missional organization to contribute in meaningful ways to the global witness of the church, Somerville did not believe in limitations imposed by ethnicity. He celebrated the organization's commitment from its inception that "the Gospel of Christ was a universal proclamation and was never intended to be restricted to or for any particular race or people. Therefore, the Lott Carey Convention is giving support to two white American Missionaries working in the Belgian Congo, also we support missionaries in China, India, Haiti and West Africa."[44] One year following the preceding statement, he would write that the organization maintained and supported "white missionaries in the Belgian Congo, yellow missionaries in China, brown missionaries in India, and black missionaries in Haiti and West Africa. A religion that is based solely upon color is unworthy of the name Christian. Therefore, the Lott Carey Baptist Foreign Mission Convention places its emphasis upon humanity regardless of race of color—this also is a unique procedure for such organizations in the past to pursue."[45]

Somerville was continuing in a bold heritage that seems ingrained in the character of the Lott Carey movement. During the 1920s, the Lott Carey Baptist Foreign Mission Society supported missionaries in Russia. A. A. Graham, Lott Carey's Corresponding Secretary, wrote in his 1923-1924 annual report of the robust vision of the Lott Carey organization and its willingness to be subjected to derision by its unconventional application of the Gospel mandate across racial lines.

> Our work in Russia constitutes a new departure, not only in the policy of our Society, but as far as I know, in the policy of all Negro Missionary Organizations in the world. In this we have dared to overstep the color line, and even rejoice in the service, not because of the petty distinction which it gives us, but because of the unlimited passion for giving the Gospel, which it manifests in our workers. No

field on earth today stands more in need of earnest help than does Russia. ... Our service to Russia may indeed be small, but no seeds were ever sown with a greater prospect of a bountiful harvest. We are glad we were called to service there, and if by the little we may do, we can relieve the distress of a single congregation, or lighten the burden of a single Christian Community, we shall rejoice and be proud of the deed. Those who either envy us, or fail to understand the scope of our sympathies, may condemn us for the part we are trying to play in the awful tragedy of this unfortunate people, but we feel honored by the privilege, and glory in the chance it gives us to demonstrate our love for humanity everywhere. ... As the Gospel of our Christ distils and envelopes this land of persecution, with its life-giving vapors, as surely it must, as time goes on, happy will be the thought that we have been instruments in the hand of God in helping to bring to pass this high and holy thing. We can bear reproach, if such exists, and endure ridicule and condemnation, if only God will permit us to march forward with the task in hand.[46]

Somerville and his wife, Alice, made an inspirational and informative pilgrimage around the world in 1960 during which he witnessed the ever present realities of racial discrimination even in international contexts.

Upon our arrival at Khartoum [Sudan] at 3:00 AM breakfast was served in the main dining room. One of the interesting scenes at this airport was the large number of people coming from and going to South Africa. One could observe on the faces of these people the marks of racial bitterness that had been stamped within the fibers of their personalities by the nefarious doctrine of apartheid. Each one seemed to resent the idea of a Negro, such as ourselves, enjoying the luxury of eating in a dining room with them. Oh well, such is life in these times![47]

While having bold convictions about the contribution to Christian foreign missions to be made by American Negroes and their African siblings, he also was clear about the racial disparities that challenged the forward progress of black people around the world. His 1960 insights about race and foreign missions with respect to a white American foreign missions sending agency reflect his concerns.

Colonial powers in Africa welcomed white missionaries while simultaneously denying visas to "American Negro Missionaries, although many of the Negro Missionaries were as well trained, and in many cases even better qualified than those of the Southern Baptist Convention." According to Somerville, many white missionaries began to look for other places for their work among black people in foreign lands as black leaders began to replace white colonialists in government. More frequent visits increased the familiarity of African leaders with the racial polemics of the United States, and their greater interaction brought deeper insights about black-white relationships around the world. Consequently, African leaders began to view missionary policies practiced by the white southerners more critically. Somerville saw the vast potential for good within the Southern Baptist Convention with its size and wealth but only if their immense resources were used to hasten freedom for African people.[48]

Somerville related a personal and distasteful experience with an Anglo American missionary culture during his 1960 visit to Nigeria that illustrated the kinds of racial challenges that hindered authentic global missional impact. Lott Carey had been prevented from entering the missionary field in Nigeria prior to its independence in 1960 because of the monopoly which some missions agencies had in this previous British territory.[49] After Nigeria's independence, Lott Carey was able to engage there with the leadership of Rev. Charles Ebong, who led the agency's work there. New opportunities were now opening to the American Negro in Nigeria.

Upon arriving in Lagos, Somerville and his wife, Alice, took a cab to a missions agency headquarters there. He asked to visit Rev. J. A. Ayorinde, whom he had met while Rev. Ayorinde and his wife were students at Virginia Union University in Richmond, Va. The missionary who greeted the Somervilles said she would call the home of Rev. and Mrs. Ayorinde. Their home adjoined the back of the agency's property. The missionary informed the Somervilles that the Ayorinde's were not at home. As the Somerville's were leaving the property, they saw Rev. Ayorinde coming out of his home. Somerville informed Ayorinde of the information he had just been given, and Ayorinde invited them into his home where his wife was seated in the living room. There may have been a reasonable explanation for the missionary's conclusion that the Ayorindes were inaccessible. Somerville, however, concluded that he had been deliberately misinformed.

After concluding their visit with the Ayorinde's, the Somervilles traveled to a Lagos hotel to wait for their Nigerian host, Rev. Charles Ebong, who had been delayed because of lengthy and difficult travel. Ebong was surprised that the white missions agency's superintendent in Lagos had not delivered an important message to the Somervilles that Ebong had asked him to relay upon their arrival. "Upon receiving this information, and recalling the seeming rebuff that I had received by the officials of the [agency] in Lagos," wrote Somerville, "I concluded that there had been 'some previous thought given' regarding the arrival of an American Negro official coming to Nigeria, which has been the [agency's] Missionary paradise."[50]

Somerville had other unpleasant experiences with the white American missionary culture in 1963. He visited Liberia along with two other Lott Carey pastor-leaders in the midst of challenges in that country.

Within recent years our program in Liberia has been punctuated by the missionaries from [a Baptist American missions agency], although it has been within the past ten years that the [Baptist American missions agency's] Missionaries have entered Liberia, they have sought through direct and indirect methods to intermeddle, and to interject themselves into the lives of our work and workers, thereby causing a constant discontent and seeking to lower the morale of our work which we have continuously carried on for the past fifty years.[51]

Fortunately, the consistent partnership of Lott Carey with their Liberian partners, the loyalty of Liberians to the Lott Carey Convention, as well as the number of Liberians who had experienced white southern American attitudes about black people, enabled Somerville's team to leave their consultation believing that "the outlook for the Lott Carey Program has never presented a greater challenge for development and expansion."[52]

Interestingly, Somerville notes two influential voices—one a U.S. evangelist and the other a British historian—that affirm his strongly held conviction about the essential role of black missionaries, despite problems of racial prejudice. Referring to a statement credited to evangelist Billy Graham upon a return from an African crusade, he cites Graham as commenting: "If the gospel of Jesus Christ is to reach the people of Africa, it must be the American Negro Missionary who must carry this message, for the people of Africa do not trust the white man regardless of his religious sincerity."[53]

Somerville's 1960 visit to Africa sharpened his understanding of the challenges of Christian missionary success on the continent. The largest liabilities to face were those related to the racism of white missionary personnel and policies. Conversations in Nigeria, where he had experienced rather blatant disregard from white missionaries, yielded sharp criticism of white missionary activities that had

deliberately disregarded all forms of human decency, and inflicted brutal and cruel acts against the defenseless people of Asia and Africa.

In talking with a group of Africans in Nigeria, they related the following: a) It was a Christian nation that invaded Ethiopia and released liquid fire upon defenseless women and children, and as these

Italian soldiers returned home they were given a heroes' reception and "blessing" by the Pope. b) The Government officials of South Africa are all in good and regular standing in the Dutch Reform Church of South Africa, also South Africa has the largest congregation of "so-called Christians" in the whole Continent of Africa. c) It was a so-called Christian nation that made and released the atomic bomb that killed and maimed 250,000 defenseless people of Japan. d) The Belgian government [responsible for brutal expressions of colonialism in Africa] represents one of the most complete Catholic countries today. e) All of the Western countries that have maintained systems of imperialism and exploitation in Africa have been so-called Christian nations.[54]

He goes on to identify the hierarchical master-servant model of white missionaries relating to black "beneficiaries." Despite the spirit of altruism possessed by some white missionaries, the racist cultural baggage that too many brought with them to Africa damaged the credibility of the Christian witness. He credited this dynamic, in part, to the effective growth of Islam in Africa. Islam claimed to offer a concept of the brotherhood of all that apparently went missing from real expressions of alleged Christians from the West into the continent.

In a searing critique of the white missionary movement in Africa through 1960, Somerville concluded "Christianity as lived and taught by Jesus Christ has not been tried in Africa. Those who have played the major role in contacting the African people have been those who have simply been vaccinated with Christianity. The greatest hindrance to Christian advancement in Africa has been racial prejudice as practiced by so-called Christians."[55] He would further argue for the unique opportunity and necessity for African American missionaries in Africa. His clarion call, however, would prove not to take root in the consciousness of the African American Christian community of the next generation.

There appears to be only one way to change this trend that is evident in Africa today, and that is for the American Negro Christian to rise up and enter into the "open door" that awaits him in Africa. Up until recent years the American Negro missionary could not secure visas to enter the areas that were under control of the Colonial powers. When we approached these Colonial officials for permission to send qualified Negro missionaries to their domain we were refused on the grounds that "Negro Missionaries are not qualified" to teach the people. Perhaps they were right in their decision, for the American Negro missionary does not conform to the pattern that Colonial powers desire in a missionary.

Certainly this is not the time nor the occasion to preach a sermon, however, it is my considered opinion that God has called the American Negro to the Kingdom at such a time as this in order that His purposes as enunciated in John, shall be fulfilled. It reads, "This Gospel of the Kingdom shall be preached in all the world and then shall the end come."

Will the American Negro Christian arise to this new challenge which is offered him to fully interpret the teaching of Christ in these newly independent countries of Africa? Perhaps time will tell.[56]

While Somerville's written reflections of the 1950s frequently referred to the climate of change and challenge in which Christian missions must precede, the 1960s saw a shift in his tone. His written reflections of the 1960s would point to revolutionary activities that saw rapid liberation of African countries from colonial oppression. The selection of mission personnel in the 1960s was done with these realities in mind. While attention to holistic work and witness was a priority in the administration of Wendell Clay Somerville, he seemed to communicate a sharper edge to this commitment through the 1960s.

Currently, the Lott Cary Convention is seeking to select, screen and appoint dedicated, intelligent and

stouthearted youth who can build civilizations as
well as build churches. ... These newly appointed
missionaries go forth fully cognizant of the recent
movement which, which took place in Addis Ababa
last May where the representatives of 90% of people
of Africa met and formed *The Organization for African
Unity*. This Conference formulated a program in
economics, finance, trade, agriculture and education,
pointing toward eventual political federation. ...
My, what a glorious challenge is offered these virile
Christian youth who go forth to join these current
African leaders in building their modern states![57]

Peace, environmental responsibility, and freedom for
all reflect a robust and holistic missional perspective that
consistently characterized Somerville's missional view for
the church and the world throughout his more than one-
half century as a missional leader. Although Somerville
had a theological, missional, and visceral predisposition
for Africa, as I stated earlier, his ethnicity did not limit his
global vision. Instead, his experience, exposure, and passion
for Africa generally helped to provide a framework through
which to see more clearly his missional mandate for the
world. Examples of country-specific insights in Africa, Asia,
and the Caribbean give deeper insight into the strategic
missional thinking of Wendell Somerville.

Ghana

Somerville believed the series of coups in Africa
during the mid 1960s was due in part to the intervention
of Western governments. The contexts of people who had
been oppressed for so many years struggling for self-
determination presented significant challenges. However,
the additional manipulative involvement of former colonial
powers yielded a volatile setting that resulted in overthrown
governments. He would write in 1966:

Behind each of these coups there has been a colonial
power that supplied arms and has encouraged these
military takeovers in order to prove two things:

a) To prove that non-white leaders are incapable of governing themselves, and b) To prevent the dark people from uniting themselves as has been envisioned by the powerful Organization of African Unity.[58]

He would further go on to discuss the overthrow of President Kwame Nkrumah of Ghana who was stigmatized by Western leaders as a Communist. Somerville believed the Western news media were following the strategy of Hitler that, "If you repeat a lie often enough people will believe it to be the truth." Somerville contended Nkrumah offended Western leaders because of his unyielding insistence that all Africans be regarded on equal terms with all other people of the world. Nkrumah demanded that people who desired to conduct business with people of Africa must allow the people fairness in decision making on issues that impacted their lives. Somerville asserted that the greatest crime of Nkrumah, trained in a Christian school and an ordained Presbyterian minister whose theology could not conceivably lead him to accept Marxist socialism's theory of materialism that some would accuse him of, was his tenacity in demanding that "all Africans must be considered as equals with all other individuals through the world regardless of race, color, or creed."[59]

South Africa

Somerville was a vehement critic of South Africa's system of apartheid and called the U.S. government, as well as other international powers, to account for their co-conspiracy in South Africa's racist policies. His 1978 assessment conveys his clear position with regard to South Africa.

Never in the history of mankind has there been a moment where man's inhumanity has been daily demonstrated than is seen in South Africa, where twenty million blacks are viciously persecuted and denied all human rights and decency by the minority whites in this southern region. While John Vorster and his murderous and criminal slaughter accelerate against defenseless blacks, we in America through pious and hypocritical rhetoric point the finger of guilt against Cuba and Russia.

Of course no Christian would seek to subscribe to the destructive policies of either of these two powers. However, God often allows non-Christians to perform acts of sympathy, concern and assistance simply because Christians fail to perform their divine assignment as commanded by our Lord Jesus Christ.[60]

He was sharply critical of Jean Kirkpatrick, U.S. Ambassador to the United Nations General Assembly, who met with General P. W. Vandeer Weshugen of South Africa's intelligence agency early in the presidency of Ronald Reagan. The U.S. government had observed a policy of not having official contact with officials of South Africa's apartheid government since 1962. Somerville concluded that this was an indication of racism being practiced at the highest levels of domestic politics because of the different responses to Kirkpatrick's "diplomacy" and that of one of her predecessors, Andrew Young. Kirkpatrick's actions and lack of official sanction starkly contradicted the punitive response to former U.S. Ambassador to the United Nations Andrew Young who conferred with a representative of the Palestine Liberation Organization in an effort to move forward the peace process in the Middle East.[61]

China

Somerville was committed to Africa, but his missional vision was larger than that. Lott Carey supported missionary efforts in China prior to the 1946-1949 rebellion led by Mao Tse-Tung to overthrow Chiang-Kai-Shek. The "tyrannical exploitation" of Chiang-Kai-Shek (who along with his wife were regarded as Christians and who was supported by "the so-called Christian people of the United States") led to the adoption of Communism in China. Rapidly, the presence of 5,000 Christian missionaries was eradicated. Despite the difficulties in China, Somerville and the Lott

Carey Convention maintained an unwavering commitment to invest in people there.

> The sympathy of the Lott Carey Convention for the masses of the people of China has been constant. As long as we were permitted to do so, we consistently supported our missionaries. Within recent months, the present regime in China has prevented us from getting funds to our missionaries. However, our faith in the Eternal God, and our love for the Chinese people convince us to "cheer up" for God has a way at times of using the forces of evil to make possible an area of good. We are further convinced that in due time we will reap in China, if we faint not.
>
> During the present interim, we are providing scholarship aide to a Chinese student in the United States. If we cannot go to the mountain, we will assist the mountain to come to us. What some people think is a total blackout in China is only an eclipse. Christ will return to China—and we are determined to assist Him to return.[62]

Bitingly, Somerville laid at the feet of Christians the rise of Communism in China when he wrote:

> For a hundred years, Christianity has had a chance to win China to Christ. However, during these hundred years the Christian church allowed the financial Moguls and political tricksters to crush the poor, friendless coolies [an ethnic slang referring to Chinese in the early 20th century], until God Almighty allowed deliverance to come to these defenseless souls through an unexpected avenue. Communism has been strong where Christians and churches have been weak in providing a means of changing unjust institutions in the interests of their victims."[63]

Somerville's concern for China was born of a tender heart for Chinese people. His missional vision, however, led him to offer political critique of manipulative international policies, particularly those of the Soviet Union and the United States. Somerville had an unfavorable assessment of the U.S. policy of not recognizing China that had nearly one—fourth of the world's population at the time. Further, China was growing in population, economics, and military capacity. It appeared to him that the U.S. position toward China was ill advised politically and would exacerbate the struggles of individuals and communities in the country. He believed had the U.S. not adopted a posture to deny the Peoples Republic of China membership in the United Nations Assembly, the U.S. would have been situated to utilize its moral influence in negotiating border disputes between China and India.[64] Despite his political posture, Somerville was consistently missional. In a radical departure from the dominant domestic political perspective of the day, Somerville would write: "The officials of the Lott Carey Convention love and respect the people of China. ... It is our sincere hope that some day we may return to Mainland China with a gospel of love and peace"[65]

India

Lott Carey initially invested in Christian missions projects in India in the 1930s then initiated ongoing programmatic support in the late 1940s that continues into the 21st Century. Somerville did not personally visit India until 1960. At that time, however, he was amazed at the effectiveness and passion of Rev. Abner and Dr. Ivey Nelson, Lott Carey's missionaries in New Delhi, who engaged in pastoral ministry and medical missions to people with leprosy. Somerville recalled:

It would be impossible for me to give a full and complete appraisal of the stupendous service which Rev. and Dr. Nelson are rendering the indigent people of India. One cannot remain in the presence of these consecrated and selfless servants of God without feeling the presence of the Holy One.

For a period of twelve years the Lott Carey Baptist Foreign Mission Convention had been making a financial expenditure for the work in [New Delhi] India. However, I did not have the faintest idea that our devoted missionaries were accomplishing so much with so little. Like Jacob of old I could say, "Surely the Lord was in this place and I knew it not." History will never fully record the deeds of love and service that are being rendered by Rev. and Mrs. Nelson and their staff of workers.[66]

Somerville was fortunate to have audiences with two Indian prime ministers. He enjoyed an audience with then Prime Minister Nehru at a reception during Somerville's 1960 visit to India. Prime Minister Indira Gandhi graciously received him in 1971. During this visit, he took great honor in presenting a check from black Christians in the United States "for the relief of the millions of homeless refugees from Bangladesh." He would record the experience in 1972:

Despite the fact that at the time of my arrival Marshal Tito of Yugoslavia was her official guest; she graciously paused to grant me an audience and expressed her deep sense of gratitude to 'my black brothers,' for their love and compassion for the ten million homeless refugees, whose lives had been crushed and threatened by the senseless warmongers.

This above experience is another demonstration of the impact that the Lott Carey Convention and its dedicated mission is having as it goes forth *Building a better world through Christian Missions* (emphasis in the original).[67]

Cuba

Somerville was consistently committed to the U.S. principles of democracy. Further, he understood the decisions of oppressed people when they chose to turn away from despots and exploiters and toward revolutionaries who sought a better way for the masses of manipulated people. An example of his interpretation of global events through his unrelenting lenses of democratic principles was his assessment of political developments in Cuba following the standoff between the U.S. and the Soviet Union under their leaders, President John F. Kennedy and Premier Nikita Khrushchev. Somerville would write in 1963: "It should forever be remembered that the present President of Cuba, Fidel Castro, was elected by the majority of the people of Cuba in 1956 as a result of the cruel and inhuman treatment which they had received at the hands of the former Dictator, Fulgencio Baptista. History has validated the fact that frustrated people in all ages have sought release and freedom from anyone who could promise hope and solace."[68]

Haiti

Somerville's analysis of the 1963 attempted *coup d'etat* in Haiti further demonstrates his commitment to principles of democracy and self-determination for nations. He asserted that the overwhelming social and economic difficulties of Haiti, combined with the lack of support of Roman Catholic priests from France who "looked askance upon the darker people of Haiti," yielded massive problems for Haiti's President Jean Jacques Duvalier. Somerville concluded race was a major influence on the insurmountable challenges to Duvalier. He believed "light skinned persons" would have been more acceptable to the Vatican and to the United States, both of whom struggled to treat with appropriate respect a black man who was president. He further commented that U.S. government officials in Washington were disappointed that the Duvalier administration was not overthrown. He also pointed to efforts made to encourage the Dominican Republic "to actively attack Haiti thereby hoping that such an attack would cause the overthrow of Dr. Duvalier's Government." Unapologetically, Somerville concluded, "The Lott Carey Baptist Foreign Mission Convention has attempted to carry on a continuous educational and missionary program among our indigent brothers of Haiti; and, we shall continue to show sympathy towards the leaders of Haiti in their struggle to raise the standards of their people."[69]

As mentioned earlier in this chapter, Wendell Somerville believed the work of missions had to be done with a keen awareness of and engagement with the broader social realities of each age. His unrelenting commitment to a holistic evangelism that sought to reveal Christ in cultures around the world, to introduce people to the transforming love of Jesus, and to make disciples in every global locale possible was expressed with sensitivity to the contextual realities with which people lived and suffered and sought to survive and thrive. It is clear to see that he viewed geopolitical and global economic developments with an unapologetic preference for the poor and the vulnerable.

Somerville had ample reason to be frustrated and defeated given the racist U.S. context in which he lived most of his life and the imperialism that hindered the authenticity of the Christian witness globally. He was clear-eyed in his assessment of the difficulties placed in the way of the effective missional strategy of his organization, as well as the Christian church around the world. Yet, he remained hopeful that his labors were not in vain, and that he and the Lott Carey Baptist Foreign Mission Convention made important contributions to the reign of God in the world.

Conclusion

African American cultural and religious tradition is mostly oral and aural. The majority of the tradition's best leaders—both historical and contemporary—communicate most frequently and most eloquently through the spoken word. Most of its religious communities likewise digest their theological lessons through hearing and subsequent dialogue. Many in this cultural milieu subscribe to the principle that words shape one's world. On the whole, people in this tradition believe in the power of words to create, empower, transform, and even destroy. They listen for emphasis, nuance, accent, cadence, inference, and more. They speak ... and listen ... and echo ... and respond. This is a powerful and defining characteristic of African American ways of being.

Like many things in most cultures, however, the greatest assets can be the greatest liabilities. The orality and aurality—commitments to speaking and hearing—of African American life have often contributed to a de-emphasis on committing ideas and insights to the written word. This particular cultural tendency combined with the obstructions of negative racial influences in the politics of the publishing world have resulted in a paucity of written resources that can enrich ourselves as well as others. Everyone is impoverished by the scarcity of African American ideas and insights committed to and distributed through the written word. This book is a modest contribution to the written reservoir of African American theological and intellectual resources that can complement the oral and aural traditions of missional leaders. This book also is a modest contribution of an African American perspective on missions which is woefully scarce throughout the discipline.

I have sought to sketch broad outlines that give some definition to the work and witness of a gifted global Christian leader whose work has brought life-giving and life-saving resources to untold numbers of people around the world. There are still layers of insight in this deep reservoir that remain to be explored and interpreted. For example, it would be interesting to explore similarities and differences of Somerville in comparison with missional practitioners of his era. What are the theological influences that shaped his missional vision and how did he evolve? How did the political observations and critiques of Somerville compare and contrast with other global Christian thinkers and/or African American thinkers of his generation? Those who take up the challenge of further examination and analysis will find many additional profound insights of this man and of the significant part of the Christian family that he represented. I hope this modest effort wets the appetites of others to taste and see that this bread is good.

Wendell Clay Somerville was unapologetically missional. His theology was grounded in his understanding that God sent God's Son to seek and to save the lost. Jesus, the Son of God, brought holistic salvation to those who would believe—spiritual, social, and physical wholeness resulted from the commitment of one's life to Jesus. Disciples of Jesus continue his work of holistic salvation as a consequence of their spiritual rebirth and transformation of life. The collection of disciples who comprise the church are obligated to intentional evangelism—taking the good news of Jesus—to the entire world, both locally and globally. The church is called to bring liberation to all who are oppressed by sin and social structures, and Christians in the United States have a particular obligation to people in the Two-Thirds World because of the affluence and opportunities available to so many in North America. African Americans cannot use their experience of racism as an excuse for missional inactivity, and Anglo Americans need to repent of their personal and institutional racism and partner with African Americans to enable a robust and effective global Christian witness.

Somerville, an African American man born in 1900, possessed an amazingly robust ecclesiology (theology of the church), soteriology (theology of salvation), Christology (theology of Jesus), and missiology (theology of missions). This book is an introduction to the missional thought of Wendell Clay Somerville, and there is much theological insight has much that commends it for those of us who live and serve in the 21st century.

I had an interesting experience with the legacy of Wendell Clay Somerville shortly after assuming leadership of the Lott Carey Baptist Foreign Mission Convention. I had gone to a church to preach and to promote investing in Christian missions around the world when an old man approached me who knew Somerville well. He said to me, "Young man, you will never fill Dr. Somerville's shoes." I replied, "You're right, sir. Dr. Somerville wears his own shoes. But I'll gladly stand on his shoulders."

Standing on the shoulders of Wendell Somerville has been my great privilege for several years. I have sought to build on his legacy just as he sought to build on the legacy of those who came before him. Somerville spoke gratefully of his honor to water seeds that others had planted. That is the responsibility of all leaders called to follow predecessors. In the world of disciples of Jesus, some plant, others water, and God gives the increase. Standing on the shoulders of Wendell Clay Somerville and watering seeds he and others have planted is what led me to write this book. I pray that his life, work, thought, and service will challenge and encourage all who read this book. I pray that this journey will help to inspire you to invest your life in Christian missions around the world. I pray that this introduction to the missiology of Wendell Clay Somerville will help to convince you that missions—sending disciples of Jesus into the world, empowered by the Holy Spirit, to touch people's lives with the transforming love of God—is essential, not optional.

The final words of this introduction to the missional thought of Wendell Clay Somerville rightfully come from his final contribution to his annual report submitted to the Lott Carey family in his retirement year of 1995 and included in the Introduction of this book.

> "My daily prayer shall be that God will ever shower his blessings upon the officials and constituents of Lott Carey and whomever my successor may be; that the mission work may be extant and spread to the far-reaching corners of the earth; that those who are faint may be stirred; that those who are willing may be directed; that those who waver may be confirmed; that wisdom and integrity may be given to all, and that all things be ordered unto God's own glory."[1]

Selected Somerville Sermons

Beginning the Year with God (2)	Genesis 1:1
Where is Your Brother Abel? (2)	Genesis 4:9
My Brother's Brother	Genesis 4:9
Saved to Save Others	Genesis 12:3
The Disturbed and the Disturbance	Genesis 21:17
The Other Mothers (2)	Genesis 21:17
Bethel	Genesis 35:3
The Ceaseless Seeker	Genesis 37:16
The Divine Command for 1963	Exodus 14:15
The Church and Her Assurances (4)	Numbers 10:29
The Marching Church	Numbers 10:29
The Meaning of the Church in the Age of Sputniks (2)	Numbers 10:29
The Divine Ultimatum	Numbers 10:29
Sharing a Divine Blessing	Numbers 10:32
A Dangerous Opportunity (3)	Numbers 13:30
A Promise Made, and A Promise Kept	Joshua 1:5
The Untrodden Way (3)	Joshua 3:4
This Strange Road	Joshua 3:4
Facing Our Jordan	Joshua 3:4
The Christian Challenge of 1964	Joshua 3:4
The Uncompleted Task (3)	Joshua 13:1
The Ceaseless Adventurer	Joshua 14:10-11
The Perpetual Adventurer	Joshua 14: 10-12
Give Me This Mountain?	Joshua 14:12

Asking God for the Impossible	Joshua 14:12
Missions or Missiles (4)	Joshua 24:15
Mothers and Missions	1 Samuel 1:28
They Stand Accused	1 Samuel 15:13-14
When Men Fail God	1 Samuel 15:13-14
Two Views of Religion	2 Kings 5:3
Choosing an Imperative Task	Nehemiah 6:3
I Am Doing a Great Work	Nehemiah 6:3
Christian Missions in These Times (2)	Esther 4:14
For Such a Time as This	Esther 4:14
Why the Heathen Rage? (2)	Psalm 2:1
God's Concern for the Heathen	Psalm 2:1, 8
A Dissatisfied Optimist	Psalm 17:15
What is Right with Foreign Missions?	Psalm 19:8
Christian Preparation for Service	Psalm 51:9-13
The Emerging Africa	Psalm 68:31
Christian Missions Now or Never	Psalm 95:7
The Good Old Days	Psalm 95:7
The Message of the Hills	Psalm 121:1
Weeping and Rejoicing	Psalm 126:6
Building a Better World through Christian Missions (2)	Psalm 127:1
Singing in a Strange Land	Psalm 137:4
The Mountaintop Church and Its Message of Salvation	Isaiah 2:2-3
Climbing Spiritual Mountains	Isaiah 2:3

Isaiah Talks to Us about One World Religion	Isaiah 2:3-4
Christian Readiness for Service	Isaiah 6:1 –10
The Ceaseless Dialogue (3)	Isaiah 6:8
When a Man Says "Yes" to God	Isaiah 6:8
The New Look in Religion	Isaiah 43:19
The Missionary Church	Isaiah 55:5
The Mission and Message of a Redeemed People (2)	Isaiah 55:5
The Church and Her Mighty Task	Isaiah 55:5
God's Spokesman in a Time of Crisis	Jeremiah 1:7
Facing the Jungle of the Jordan (4)	Jeremiah 12:5
The Child of God Who Can't Quit	Jeremiah 20:9
God Still Answers Prayer	Jeremiah 29:12
A Word from the Lord (11)	Jeremiah 37:17
Those Who Pass By	Lamentations 1:12
New Hearts for '54	Ezekiel 36:26
Message from the Book of Jonah to Our Generation (3)	Jonah 4:10-11
Who is Jonah?	Jonah 4:10-11
Let Us Consider Jonah	Jonah 4:10-11
A Minor Prophet with a Major Message	Micah 6:4
Spiritual Power for '55	Zechariah 4:6
God's Secret Power	Zechariah 4:6
Thou Shall Call His Name Jesus	Matt. 1:21
The Eternal Search and Discovery	Matt. 2:2

Christ, The Born King	Matt. 2:2
Wise Men Seek the Born King	Matt. 2:2
The Quest Of The Wise Men	Matt. 2:2
On Becoming A "Real" Man	Matt. 4:19
Happiness Found Through Universal Service	Matt. 5:6
Extraordinary Christians In These Times	Matt. 5:47
Folks Who Are Different	Matt. 5:47
Heavenly Treasuries	Matt. 6:19-21
Spiritual Investors	Matt. 6:19-21
First Things First	Matt. 6:33
A Time Of Testing Our Religion	Matt. 7:12, Acts 10:34
Who Call Me Christian?	Matt. 7:13-23
The Great Calm	Matt. 8:26
A Sublime Partnership	Matt. 9:37
The Plenteous Harvest	Matt. 9:37-38
The Spiritual Task Of God And Man	Matt. 9:37
When Men Become Uncertain About God	Matt. 11:3
The Church And Her Mission	Matt. 11:4
Shall We Send Them Away?	Matt. 14:15
What About Jesus?	Matt. 16:15
Conditions of Discipleship	Matt. 16:24
A Voice From The Summit	Matt: 17:5
The Christ Of The Ages	Matt. 17:8
Asking God For The Impossible	Matt. 19:26
Who Is This King?	Matt. 21:10
This Gospel	Matt. 24:14
A Time of Testing	Matt. 25:40
The Least of These	Matt. 25:40
The Least of These	Matt. 25:45
The World's Greatest Question	Matt. 27:22
What About Jesus And Foreign Missions?	Matt. 27:22
The World's Greatest Question Today	Matt. 27:22

The Risen Christ	Matt. 28:6
The Divine Assignment	Matt. 28:16—20
Triumphal Faith in an Age of Doubt	Matt. 28:17
But Some Doubted	Matt. 28:18
Why Me?	Matt. 28:19
Where Do You Think You're Going?	Matt. 28:18-20
A Divine Command and An Eternal Promise	Matt. 28:19-20
The Blueprint of God's World Plan	Matt. 28:20
The Great Adventure	Mark 1:17
The Christian Joy of Becoming	Mark 1:17
Life's Sure Way to Become Somebody	Mark 1:17
The Challenged Christ	Mark 1:24
That Which All Men Seek	Mark 1:37
When Men Find Christ	Mark 1:37-38
The Unrestricted Christ	Mark 1:38
A Special Assignment—Meeting the Needs of Others	Mark 1:38
Asking God for the Impossible	Mark 1:40
Faith Rewarded	Mark 1:40
When the Impossible Becomes the Possible	Mark 1:40
Christ's Answer is "Yes"	Mark 1:41
The Other Side of the Lake	Mark 4:35
A Participant in an Extraordinary Event	Mark 4:35
What About Jesus in a Tangled World	Mark 4:41
Whose Business Is It? (6)	Mark 5:7
Saved for an End	Mark 5:19
Shall We Send Them Away? (3)	Mark 6:35-36
The Message of the Multitudes	Mark 6:34-44
The Christian's Belief in Missions	Mark 9:24
What a Certain Baptist Believes	Mark 9:24
A Marvelous Discovery	Mark 9:8

The Great Failure	Mark 10:22
The Role of the American Negro Christian	Mark 15:21
The Role of the Contemporary Black Church	Mark 15:21
The Role of the Contemporary Black Church and Missions	Mark 15:21
The Whole Church Preaching the Whole Gospel to The Whole World	Mark 16:15
How Big Is Your "All the World"?	Mark 16:15
Signs That Follow Faithfulness	Mark 16:20
How Far Is Your Everywhere? (7)	Mark 16:20
God Confirms His Promises	Mark 16:20
Jesus	Luke 1:31
Youth And God's Work	Luke 2:49
An Inside Message for an Outside Service	Luke 4:18
Christ Proclaims His Divine Assignment	Luke 4:18-19
The Greater Society Proclaimed and Fulfilled	Luke 4:21
The Fulfilled Assignment	Luke 4:21
A Religion That Proclaims and Performs	Luke 4:21
Fulfilling a Divine Assignment	Luke 4:43
A Special Assignment	Luke 4:43
Doing Something Special for God	Luke 4:43
They Who Follow Christ	Luke 5:11
The Inquiry of the "Concerned" Christian	Luke 7:19
When Men Become Uncertain about God	Luke 7:19
The Christ of 1945	Luke 7:19
Mankind Wants an Answer	Luke 7:20
Christ Has the Answer	Luke 7:20
The Way to True Happiness	Luke 7:23
The Other Side of the Lake (4)	Luke 8:22
What Happens When You Take Jesus Seriously	Luke 8:22

Traveling with Jesus as Our Companion	Luke 8:22
A Divine Compulsion	Luke 9:16
The Road of Most Resistance	Luke 9:51
The Steadfast Christ	Luke 9:51
Majoring on Minors	Luke 9:60
Our Glorious Privileges	Luke 10:23-24
Church Work or the Work of the Church	Luke 10:25-37
The Church's Divine Assignmen	Luke 10:37
The Missing Nine	Luke 17:17
The Grateful Minority	Luke 17:18
A Religion That Saves	Luke 19:10
The Things That Make for Peace	Luke 19:42
I Have Found No Fault in Jesus	Luke 23:4
The New Role of the American Negro Christian	Luke 23:26
The Glorious Remembrance	Luke 24:8
Christ the Eternal Light (4)	John 1:5
The Light That Shall Never Fail	John 1:5
The Unextinguished Light	John 1:5
The Universal Proclamation	John 2:5
God's Love Expressed through His Gift	John 3:16
The Divine Must (2)	John 4:4
A Divine Imperative	John 4:4
If You Knew (3)	John 4:10
The Significance of the Insignificant	John 4:39–42
The Voice of Hope	John 5:6
Wholeness is Found through Christ	John 5:6
Freedom through Christ	John 8:32-36
Freedom	John 8:36
The Other Sheep	John 10:16
God's Other Sheep	John 10:16
The Master is Come and Calleth for Thee	John 11:28

Seeking Jesus	John 12:21
The Ceaseless Search	John 12:21, 20:13
On Becoming a Good Minister of Jesus Christ	John 12:26
The Greater Works Than These	John 14:12
Why Christian Missionaries Go Forth	John 14:12; 17:18
The Challenge of Christian Missions	John 17:18
The Divine Assignment	John 17:18
When Leaders Go Fishing	John 21:3
Foreign Missionaries Are Coming to Town	John 21:15
The Church Faces a Time of Testing	John 21:15
Making Christ the Object of Our Love and Devotion	John 21:15
Look Who's Coming to Norfolk	John 21:15
The All Important "After" Experience	Acts 1:8
The Good Witness of Jesus Christ	Acts 1:8
After Easter, What?	Acts 1:8
When Religion Had Power	Acts 3:1-8
The Role of the Church in a Time of Need	Acts 3:5
What's the Payoff? (2)	Acts 3:5
What Others Expect of Christians (2)	Acts 3:5
Jesus, The Divine Ultimate	Acts 4:12
The Church in Action	Acts 5:41-42
The Ceaseless Gospel	Acts 5:42
The Christian Layman and Tomorrow's World	Acts 8:1
Jerusalem Christians	Acts 8:14
The Way of the Missionaries	Acts 8:26
Two Men and A Vision	Acts 10:2-4
An Understanding Religion	Acts 10:34-35
The First Church (2)	Acts 11:26
The New Testament Church (2)	Acts 11:26

The Mission of the Church in the World	Acts 11:26
Why Turn to the Gentiles?	Acts 13:46
What God Expects of His Church (2)	Acts 13:47
The Christian Responsibility	Acts 13:47
The Global Assignment of the Church	Acts 15:16
Re-Thinking Our Foreign Mission Task (2)	Acts 15:36
The Man of Troas	Acts 16:8
The Vision of Troas	Acts 16:8
The Call of God	Acts 16:9
Sharing Your Religion	Acts:16:9-10
The Divine Call and the Human Response	Acts 16:9-10
The Call from Abroad	Acts 16:9-10
On Being in a Hurry for God	Acts 16:10
A Shared Vision	Acts 16:10
On Straight Course to Philippi	Acts 16:12
The Church in Trouble	Acts 16:30
Who Wants to Be Saved?	Acts 16:30
Thermostat Christians	Acts 17:6
A Disturbing Religion (2)	Acts 17:7
This is What Jesus Did for Me	Acts 26:15-16
Obeying the Best (2)	Acts 26:19
The Voice of God's Man in Times of Crisis	Acts 27:25
Sufficient Evidence to Convict	Romans 1:8
Christian Readiness	Romans 1:15
The Honest Debtor	Romans 1:17
The Unanswered Inquiry	Romans 10:14-15
The Inquiry of the Concerned Christian	Romans 10:14-16
Laborers with God	1 Corinthians 3:9

Our More Than Enough and Our Neighbors Less Than Enough	2 Corinthians 8:14
Spiritual Endurance	Galatians 6:9
Faithfulness Rewarded	1 Thessalonians 1:8
God Works through Those Who Believe	1 Thessalonians 2:13
The Good Minister of Jesus Christ	1 Timothy 4:6
Some Steps toward Success in 1966	2 Timothy 1:13
I Have Kept the Faith	2 Timothy 4:7
The Great Contest (4)	2 Timothy 4:7
Religion at Its Best	Hebrews 11:24-26
Making an Unpopular Choice	Hebrews 11: 24-46
The Changeless Christ in a Changeless World	Hebrews 13:8
The Religion of the Open Door (5)	Revelation 3:8
A Church that Met God's Test (3)	Revelation 3:8
The Church Faces Armageddon	Revelation 16:16

Notes

Foreword

[1]Sandy D. Martin, <u>Black Baptists and African Missions: The Origins of a Movement 1880-1915</u> (Macon, GA: Mercer University Press, 1989), 1.

[2]William Brackney, <u>The Baptists</u> (New York: Greenwood Press, 1988), 139-140.

Introduction

[1]Wendell C. Somerville, <u>Annual Report of the Executive Secretary</u> (Washington, DC: Lott Carey Baptist Foreign Mission Convention, 1946 – 1947), p. 3.

[2]Wendell C. Somerville, <u>Annual Report of the Executive Secretary</u> (Washington, DC: Lott Carey Baptist Foreign Mission Convention, 1989 – 1990), p. 3.

[3]Wendell C. Somerville, <u>Official Report on Visit to the Foreign Field: December 4, 1947 – February 4, 1948 to the Executive Committee of Lott Carey Baptist Foreign Mission Convention U.S.A.</u> (Washington, DC: Lott Carey Baptist Foreign Mission Convention, 1948), p. 20.

[4]Ibid., p. 24 – 25.

[5]Wendell C. Somerville, <u>Annual Report of the Executive Secretary</u> (Washington, DC: Lott Carey Baptist Foreign Mission Convention, 1942 – 1943), p. 9.

[6]Wendell C. Somerville, <u>Annual Report of the Executive Secretary</u> (Washington, DC: Lott Carey Baptist Foreign Mission Convention, 1949 – 1950), p. 4.

[7]Wendell C. Somerville, <u>Around the World for "Others"</u> (Washington, DC: Lott Carey Baptist Foreign Mission Convention, 1961), p. 45.

[8]Wendell C. Somerville, <u>Annual Report of the Executive Secretary</u> (Washington, DC: Lott Carey Baptist Foreign Mission Convention, 1987 – 1988), p. 3.

[9]Wendell C. Somerville, <u>Annual Report of the Executive Secretary</u> (Washington, DC: Lott Carey Baptist Foreign Mission Convention, 1994 – 1995), p. 11.

The Missional Church

[1]"The Mission of the Church in the World"
[2]"The Challenged Christ"
[3]"The Message of the Multitudes"
[4]"The Missionary Church"
[5]"The Good Witness of Jesus Christ"
[6]"The Church in Action"
[7]"Re-Thinking our Foreign Mission Task"
[8]Ibid.
[9]"Jerusalem Christians"
[10]Ibid.
[11]Ibid.
[12]<u>Biography of Elder Lott Cary, Late Missionary to Africa. With an Appendix on the Subject of Colonization,</u> by J.H.B. Latrobe, J. B. Taylor, Baltimore: Armstrong & Berry. J. W. Woods, 1837, pp. 24 – 25.
[13]"The Vision of Troas"

[14]"The World's Greatest Question Today"
[15]"Foreign Missionaries Are Coming to Town"
[16]"Those Who Pass By"
[17]"The First Church"
[18]"The New Testament Church"
[19]Ibid.
[20]"Who is Jonah?"
[21]"The Christian Challenge of 1964"
[22]"What's the Payoff?"
[23]"Jesus"
[24]"The Inquiry of the 'Concerned' Christian"
[25]"The Church's Divine Assignment"
[26]"Majoring in Minors"
[27]"Fulfilling A Divine Assignment"
[28]"The Christ of 1945"
[29]"Doing Something for God"
[30]"A Disturbing Religion"
[31]"The Inquiry of the 'Concerned' Christian
[32]"A Disturbing Religion"
[33]"The Church And Her Mission"
[34]Ibid.
[35]Ibid.
[36]"Youth and God's Work"
[37]"The Church in Trouble"
[38]" The Church Faces a Time of Testing"
[39]"When Leaders Go Fishing"
[40]"This Gospel"
[41]"Happiness Found through Universal Service"
[42]"The Changeless Christ in a Changing World"
[43]"Faithfulness Rewarded"
[44]"Christian Missions in These Times"
[45]"For Such a Time as This"
[46]"When Men Find Christ"
[47]"What About Jesus in a Tangled World"
[48]"The Message of the Multitudes"
[49]"Making an Unpopular Choice"
[50]"Why Turn to the Gentiles?"
[51]Wendell C. Somerville, <u>Annual Report of the Executive Secretary</u> (Washington, DC: Lott Carey Baptist Foreign Mission Convention, 1946 – 1947), p. 9.
[52]Wendell C. Somerville, <u>Annual Report of the Executive Secretary</u> (Washington, DC: Lott Carey Baptist Foreign Mission Convention, 1982 – 1983), p. 3.
[53]Wendell C. Somerville, <u>Annual Report of the Executive Secretary</u> (Washington, DC: Lott Carey Baptist Foreign Mission Convention, 1946 – 1947), p. 8.
[54]Wendell C. Somerville, <u>Annual Report of the Executive Secretary</u> (Washington, DC: Lott Carey Baptist Foreign Mission Convention, 1975 – 1976), p. 4.
[55]Wendell C. Somerville, <u>Annual Report of the Executive Secretary</u> (Washington, DC: Lott Carey Baptist Foreign Mission Convention, 1980 – 1981), pp. 4 – 5.
[56]"The Church in Action"
[57]"A Time Of Testing"
[58]"The Unanswered Inquiry"
[59]"Who Wants to Be Saved?"
[60]"Missiles or Missions"
[61]Ibid.
[62]"Mothers and Missions"
[63]"Asking God For The Impossible"

[64]When Little Rock, Arkansas sought to integrate Little Rock Central High School with the admission of nine Negro students in 1957, Governor Orval Faubus mobilized the state's National Guard to prevent the children from entering the school. His actions were overturned by a federal judge and President Dwight D. Eisenhower federalized the National Guard, removing the students from the governor's authority. As the children entered the school a few days later, hundreds of people who opposed integration surrounded the school, intimidating the children and the school personnel. Shortly thereafter, with the protection of army troops, the nine children were allowed to enter. They finished that first school year with one of the nine in the graduating class.

[65]Wendell C. Somerville, <u>Annual Report of the Executive Secretary</u> (Washington, DC: Lott Carey Baptist Foreign Mission Convention, 1956 – 1957), p. 4.

[66]"Saved to Save Others"

[67]"A Dangerous Opportunity"

[68]"This Strange Road"

[69]"The Role of the American Negro Christian"

[70]Wendell C. Somerville, Annual Report of the Executive Secretary-Treasurer, (Washington, DC: Lott Carey Baptist Foreign Mission Convention, 1968 – 1969, p. 2.

[71]"The Role of the Contemporary Black Church"

[72]Ibid.

[73]"The Role of the Contemporary Black Church and Missions"

[74]"Church Work or the Work of the Church"

[75]"The Church in Action"

[76]"A Religion That Proclaims and Performs"

The Missional Life

[1]"The Greater Works than These!"

[2]"A Religion That Seeks and Saves"

[3]Ibid.

[4]"Foreign Missionaries Are Coming to Town"

[5]Ibid.

[6]"The Spiritual Task of God and Man"

[7]"The Unrestricted Christ"

[8]"The Light That Never Fails"

[9]"The Light That Never Fails"

[10]"When Men Become Uncertain About God"

[11]The World's Greatest Question

[12]"What about Jesus and Foreign Missions?"

[13]"The Risen Christ"

[14]"Where Do You Think You're Going?"

[15]"Christian Readiness"

[16]"If You Knew"

[17]"Re-Thinking our Foreign Mission Task"

[18]"Freedom through Christ"

[19]"The Eternal Search and Discovery"

[20]"God's Other Sheep"

[21]"If You Knew"

[22]The Quest of the Wise Men

[23]On Becoming a "Real" Man

[24]The Spiritual Task of God and Man

[25]"Christ, The Born King"

[26]"The Ceaseless Dialogue"

[27]"An Inside Message for an Outside Service"

[28]"The Way to True Happiness"
[29]"They Who Follow Christ"
[30]"The Church's Divine Assignment"
[31]"Mankind Wants an Answer"
[32]"The Things That Make for Peace"
[33]Ibid.
[34]"The Master is Come and Calleth for Thee"
[35]"Choosing an Imperative Task"
[36]"The Divine Call and the Human Response"
[37]"Laborers with God"
[38]"The Glorious Remembrance"
[39]"The Church's Divine Assignment"
[40]"Christ Proclaims His Divine Assignment"
[41]"The Other Side of the Lake"
[42]"The Grateful Minority"
[43]Ibid.
[44]A Religion That Seeks and Saves
[45]"Asking God for the Impossible"
[46]"Give Me This Mountain?"
[47]"Life's Sure Way to Become Somebody"
[48]"The Challenged Christ"
[49]"The Other Side of the Lake"
[50]"The Great Adventure"
[51]"The Church And Her Mission"
[52]"What about Jesus and Christian Missions?"
[53]"Whose Business Is It?"
[54]"The Christian's Belief in Missions"
[55]"How Far is Your Everywhere?"
[56]Ibid.
[57]"A Divine Imperative"
[58]"Message from the Book of Jonah to Our Generation"
[59]"Christian Missions Now or Never"
[60]"Building a Better World through Christian Missions"
[61]"Conditions of Discipleship"
[62]"What about Jesus and Christian Missions?"
[63]"Why Me?"

The Missional Strategy

[1]Wendell C. Somerville, Annual Report of the Executive Secretary (Washington, DC: Lott Carey Baptist Foreign Mission Convention, 1956 – 1957), p. 3.

[2]Wendell C. Somerville, Annual Report of the Executive Secretary (Washington, DC: Lott Carey Baptist Foreign Mission Convention, 1961 – 1962), p. 4.

[3]Wendell C. Somerville, Annual Report of the Executive Secretary (Washington, DC: Lott Carey Baptist Foreign Mission Convention, (1972 – 1973), pp. 3 – 4.

[4]Wendell C. Somerville, Annual Report of the Executive Secretary (Washington, DC: Lott Carey Baptist Foreign Mission Convention, 1945 – 1946), p. 7.

[5]Wendell C. Somerville, Annual Report of the Executive Secretary (Washington, DC: Lott Carey Baptist Foreign Mission Convention, 1942 – 1943), pp. 3 – 5.

[6]Wendell C. Somerville, Lott Carey: Seventy-Three Years as the Perpetual Convention of Distinction (Washington, DC: Lott Carey Baptist Foreign Mission Convention, 1971), pp. 50 – 55.

[7]Wendell C. Somerville, Annual Report of the Executive Secretary (Washington, DC: Lott Carey Baptist Foreign Mission Convention, 1940 – 1941), p. 5.

[8]Ibid., p. 14.

[9]Wendell C. Somerville, Annual Report of the Executive Secretary (Washington, DC: Lott Carey Baptist Foreign Mission Convention, 1976 – 1977), pp. 2 – 3.

[10]Wendell C. Somerville, Annual Report of the Executive Secretary (Washington, DC: Lott Carey Baptist Foreign Mission Convention, 1984 – 1985), p. 3.

[11]Wendell C. Somerville, Annual Report of the Executive Secretary (Washington, DC: Lott Carey Baptist Foreign Mission Convention, 1943 – 1944), pp. 7 – 8.

[12]Wendell C. Somerville, Official Report on Visit to the Foreign Field: December 4, 1947 – February 4, 1948 to the Executive Committee of Lott Carey Baptist Foreign Mission Convention U.S.A. (Washington, DC: Lott Carey Baptist Foreign Mission Convention, 1948), p. 4.

[13]Wendell C. Somerville, Annual Report of the Executive Secretary (Washington, DC: Lott Carey Baptist Foreign Mission Convention, 1956 – 1957), p. 3.

[14]Wendell C. Somerville, Annual Report of the Executive Secretary (Washington, DC: Lott Carey Baptist Foreign Mission Convention, 1970 – 1971), p. 2.

[15]Wendell C. Somerville, "What Is Central in the Lott Carey Program," in Lott Carey…The Convention of Distinction: Fifty-Five Years of Ceaseless Service to Others (Washington, DC: Lott Carey Baptist Foreign Mission Convention, 1953), p. 54.

[16]Wendell C. Somerville, Annual Report of the Executive Secretary (Washington, DC: Lott Carey Baptist Foreign Mission Convention, 1945 – 1946), p. 9.

[17]Wendell C. Somerville, "What Is Central in the Lott Carey Program," p. 56.

[18]Ibid.

[19]"Asking God for the Impossible"

[20]Wendell C. Somerville, Annual Report of the Executive Secretary (Washington, DC: Lott Carey Baptist Foreign Mission Convention, 1986 – 1987), p. 5

[21]Wendell C. Somerville, Annual Report of the Executive Secretary (Washington, DC: Lott Carey Baptist Foreign Mission Convention, 1940 – 1941), p. 4.

[22]Wendell C. Somerville, Annual Report of the Executive Secretary (Washington, DC: Lott Carey Baptist Foreign Mission Convention, 1949 – 1950), p. 3.

[23]Wendell C. Somerville, Annual Report of the Executive Secretary (Washington, DC: Lott Carey Baptist Foreign Mission Convention, 1949 – 1950) p. 4.

[24]Ibid., p. 3.

[25]Ibid., p. 4.

[26]Wendell C. Somerville, Annual Report of the Executive Secretary (Washington, DC: Lott Carey Baptist Foreign Mission Convention, 1985 – 1986), p. 3.

[27]Wendell C. Somerville, Annual Report of the Executive Secretary (Washington, DC: Lott Carey Baptist Foreign Mission Convention, 1945 – 1946), pp. 8 – 9.

[28]Wendell C. Somerville, Annual Report of the Executive Secretary (Washington, DC: Lott Carey Baptist Foreign Mission Convention, 1950 – 1951, p. 3.

[29]Ibid., p. 6.

[30]Wendell C. Somerville, Annual Report of the Executive Secretary (Washington, DC: Lott Carey Baptist Foreign Mission Convention, 1958 – 1959), pp. 3 – 4.

[31]Ibid., pp. 5, 7.

[32]Wendell C. Somerville, Around the World for "Others" (Washington, DC: Lott Carey Baptist Foreign Mission Convention, 1961), p. 11.

[33]Ibid., p. 13.

[34]Ibid., pp. 15 – 16.

[35]Ibid., p. 20.

[36]Ibid., pp. 26 – 27.

[37]Wendell C. Somerville, Annual Report of the Executive Secretary (Washington, DC: Lott Carey Baptist Foreign Mission Convention, 1962 – 1963), p. 6.

[38]Ibid., pp. 6 – 7.

[39]Wendell C. Somerville, Annual Report of the Executive Secretary (Washington, DC: Lott Carey Baptist Foreign Mission Convention, 1963 – 1964), p. 1.

[40]Wendell C. Somerville, Annual Report of the Executive Secretary (Washington, DC: Lott Carey Baptist Foreign Mission Convention, 1940 – 1941), p. 13.

[41]Ibid., p. 15.

[42]Wendell C. Somerville, Annual Report of the Executive Secretary (Washington, DC: Lott Carey Baptist Foreign Mission Convention, 1949 – 1950), p, 5.

[43]U. S. Census Bureau Historical Income Tables http://www.census.gov/hhes/www/income/histinc/f05.html

[44]Wendell C. Somerville, Annual Report of the Executive Secretary (Washington, DC: Lott Carey Baptist Foreign Mission Convention, 1944 – 1945), p. 3.

[45]Wendell C. Somerville, Annual Report of the Executive Secretary (Washington, DC: Lott Carey Baptist Foreign Mission Convention, 1945 – 1946), p. 3.

[46]A. A. Graham, Annual Report of the Corresponding Secretary (Washington, DC: Lott Carey Baptist Foreign Mission Society, 1923 – 1924), pp. 28 – 29.

[47]Wendell C. Somerville, Around the World for "Others" (Washington, DC: Lott Carey Baptist Foreign Mission Convention, 1961), pp. 23 – 24.

[48]Ibid., p. 17.

[49]Wendell C. Somerville, Annual Report of the Executive Secretary (Washington, DC: Lott Carey Baptist Foreign Mission Convention, 1962 – 1963), p. 8

[50]Wendell C. Somerville, Around the World for "Others" (Washington, DC: Lott Carey Baptist Foreign Mission Convention, 1961), p. 21.

[51]Wendell C. Somerville, Annual Report of the Executive Secretary (Washington, DC: Lott Carey Baptist Foreign Mission Convention, 1962 – 1963), p. 7

[52]Ibid.

[53]Wendell C. Somerville, Annual Report of the Executive Secretary (Washington, DC: Lott Carey Baptist Foreign Mission Convention, 1959 – 1960), p. 7.

[54]Wendell C. Somerville, Around the World for "Others" (Washington, DC: Lott Carey Baptist Foreign Mission Convention, 1961), p. 27 – 28.

[55]Ibid., p. 28.

[56]Ibid., 28 – 29.

[57]Wendell C. Somerville, Annual Report of the Executive Secretary (Washington, DC: Lott Carey Baptist Foreign Mission Convention, 1963 – 1964), pp. 3 – 4.

[58]Wendell C. Somerville, Annual Report of the Executive Secretary (Washington, DC: Lott Carey Baptist Foreign Mission Convention, 1965 – 1966), p. 3.

[59]Ibid., p. 5.

[60]Wendell C. Somerville, Annual Report of the Executive Secretary (Washington, DC: Lott Carey Baptist Foreign Mission Convention, 1977 – 1978), p. 3.

[61]Wendell C. Somerville, Annual Report of the Executive Secretary (Washington, DC: Lott Carey Baptist Foreign Mission Convention, 1980 – 1981), p. 5.

[62]Wendell C. Somerville, Annual Report of the Executive Secretary (Washington, DC: Lott Carey Baptist Foreign Mission Convention, 1952 – 1953), pp. 5, 7.

[63]Wendell C. Somerville, Annual Report of the Executive Secretary (Washington, DC: Lott Carey Baptist Foreign Mission Convention 1949 – 1950), pp. 3 – 4.

[64]Wendell C. Somerville, Annual Report of the Executive Secretary (Washington, DC: Lott Carey Baptist Foreign Mission Convention, 1962 – 1963), p. 4 – 5.

[65]Wendell C. Somerville, Annual Report of the Executive Secretary (Washington, DC: Lott Carey Baptist Foreign Mission Convention, 1959 – 1960), p. 4.

[66]Wendell C. Somerville, Around the World for "Others" (Washington, DC: Lott Carey Baptist Foreign Mission Convention, 1961), p. 37.

[67]Wendell C. Somerville, Annual Report of the Executive Secretary (Washington, DC: Lott Carey Baptist Foreign Mission Convention, 1971 – 1972), p. 6.

[68]Wendell C. Somerville, Annual Report of the Executive Secretary (Washington, DC: Lott Carey Baptist Foreign Mission Convention, 1962 – 1963), p. 3.

[69]Ibid., p. 4.

Conclusion

[1]Wendell C. Somerville, Annual Report of the Executive Secretary (Washington, DC: Lott Carey Baptist Foreign Mission Convention, 1994 – 1995), p. 11.

Index

www.ingramcontent.com/pod-product-compliance
Lightning Source LLC
Chambersburg PA
CBHW030514100426
42813CB00001B/43